Publishing Children's Poetry For 19 Years

Giving verse a voice

Essex

Edited by Jenni Bannister & Helen Davies

First published in Great Britain in 2010 by:

Young Writers
Remus House
Coltsfoot Drive
Peterborough
PE2 9JX
Telephone: 01733 890066
Website: www.youngwriters.co.uk

All Rights Reserved
Book Design by Spencer Hart, Ali Smith & Tim Christian
© Copyright Contributors 2009
SB ISBN 978-1-84924-796-2

Foreword

Young Writers' Bust-A-Rhyme competition is a showcase for secondary school pupils to share their poetic creativity and inspiration. Selecting the poems has been challenging and immensely rewarding. The effort and imagination invested by these young writers makes their poems a pleasure to enjoy reading time and time again.

Young Writers was established in 1991 to nurture creativity in our children and young adults, to give them an interest in poetry and an outlet to express themselves. Seeing their work in print will encourage them to keep writing and become our poets of tomorrow.

Contents

Anglo European School
Lea Wood (12) 1
Aleyna Costin (11) 2
Amy Morgan (17) 2
Maisie Allen (12) 3
Jessica Green (12) 3
Tobias Clark (14) 4
Tamarra Atkinson (11) 4
Neville Firattan (12) 5
Conrad Stace (12) 5
Olukorede Banjo (12) 6

Barking Abbey Comprehensive Upper School
Aniqa Riba & Kajal Dhingra (11) 6
Lybah Kiran (11) 7
Whitney Goold-Walters (11) 8
Megan McDermott (12) 9
Maisie Crowley (12) 9
Manisha Juttla (12) 10
Ellie Rouse (11) 10
Karan Singh Ahir (11) 11
Sabiha Rahman Chowdhury (12) 11
Rahid Ahmed (12) 12
Hadisa Rehman (11) 12
Hashim Mahmood (12) 13
Harry Murphy (11) 13
Shivani Rajput (11) 14
Adiba Begum 14
Amy Stainsbury (11) 15
Lemmar Reid (11) 15
Tehseen Ahmad (11) 16
Karim Benotmane (11) 16
Luckvir Bhati 17
Shibaz Hussain 17
Jannat Rashad (11) 17
Zoe Chafer (11) 18

Chase High School
Abbie Kinerman (14) 18
Emma Turner 19

Michael Berry (14) 20
Charlotte Tanner (11) 20
Abbie MacGavin (14) 21
Cameron Russell (12) 21
Charlie Ward 22
Joe Lawrence (14) 22
Jay Duncumb (14) 23
Julia Cichocka (11) 23
Robert Elliott 24
Dominic Glatter (14) 24
Sarah Weaver (11) 25
Daniella Hare (11) 25
Alexander De Boick (11) 25
Bertha Sibanda (11) 26
Sajada Rahman (11) 26
Josh Hindle (14) 27
Paige Elcoate (11) 27

Children's Support Service
Terry Higgins (15) 27
Havannah Withey (15) 28
Daniel Hill (15) 29
Alfie Lawrence (15) 29

Clacton County High School
Hannah Clarke (12) 30
Molly Blake (12) 31
Amber Bellinger (12) 32
Siobhan Tillyer (12) 33

King Edward VI Grammar School
C J Mayes (12) 33
Mainak Datta (13) 34
Kurian George (12) 34
James Beaumont (12) 35

Kingswode Hoe School
Aaron Holness (11) 35
Ellie Longman (11) 36
Bailey Saunders (11) 36
Jessica Blake (11) 37
Caleb Baccarini (11) 37

Corey Byrne (11) 38
Jodie Lawrence (11) 38
Jake Candler (11) 39
Emma Rawling (11) 39
Georgina Mobbs (11)........................... 40
Jordan Shults (12) 40
Bruno Simoes Da Cruz (11).................. 41
Gareth Brady (11) 41

Maltings Academy
Joseph McGee (12)............................. 41
Adam Piper (12) 42
George Hull (12) 42
Tommy King (12) 43
Thomas Johnson (12)........................... 43
Mark Mead (12) 44
Sam English (12)................................. 44

Ormiston Park Academy
Lorenzo Korta-Haupt
& Benjamin Smith (12) 45
Jaye Willams (12)................................. 45
Tiffany Ruane (12)
& Samantha Joe Martin (13) 46
Nicola Lewis (13).................................. 46
Lauren Ward (12) 47
Natasha Louise Smith (12).................... 47
Scarlet Anderson (12)........................... 48
Beth Fisk (12) 48
Kara Cross & Molly Russell (12)............. 49
Caitlin Harmony Rice (12) 49
Simone Georgia Hibbert (12)................. 50
Sharon Sangotade (12) 50
Luke Capstick (12)................................ 51
Aaron Agyekum (12)............................. 51
Chloe Ferguson (12)............................. 52
Fern Skingley (12) 52

Park School for Girls
Jadesola Olopade (14) 52
Sehyr Sarfaraz (12) 53
Dilshad Adam (12)................................ 54
Aaliya Farook Oomerjee (12) 55
Soha Nadeem (11) 55
Harini Anand (13).................................. 56
Maria Farook Oomerjee (13) 56

Sophie Caruana (13) 57
Sabrina Fearon Melville (11).................. 57
Warner Dixon (12) 58
Rohini Soni (14).................................... 58
Saffiyah Omar (12) 59
Saleha Ahmed (12)............................... 59
Prabhjot Kaur (12) 60
Shayla Reid (12)................................... 60
Ammarah Wali (12)............................... 61
Monisha Mehta (12).............................. 61
Caroline Cheung (13) 62
Karishma Desai (11)............................. 62
Simran Dev (12) 63
Sara Siabi (13)..................................... 63
Shashiwadana Kariyakarawana (14)..... 64
Mahham Mukhtar (13) 64
Zara Kaur (13) 65
Rumaanah Sajid Tailor (13)................... 65
Mica Mehta (12)................................... 66
Vrindha Venn (13)................................ 66
Shreyashi Verma (12)........................... 67
Sana Patel (12).................................... 67

Redden Court School
Emily Henderson (12)........................... 68
Harry Rogers (12)................................. 69
Georgina Martin (13) 69
Chelsea Huggins (13)........................... 70
Gemma Brooks (13) 70
Sarah Eost (12) 71
Chloe Wade (13) 71
Megan Brown (12)................................ 72
Sean Nicolaides (11) 72
Emily Hart (12)..................................... 73
Karis Davey (13).................................. 73
Heather Eldridge (12) 74
Danielle Aubrey-Tootell (12) 74
Joseph Brewer (12).............................. 75
Ria Smyth (11)..................................... 75
Louise Garraway (12)........................... 76
Sean Callum Jacks (11)........................ 76
Jessica Russell (12) 77
Chloe Palmer-Anscomb (11) 77
Louie Hak (12) 78
Ben Hunt (11) 78

Sophy Bakal (13)	79
Jack Collins (14)	79
Shannon Barrett (12)	80
Georgina Newland (12)	80
Adam Hewitt (13)	81
Lewis Jaggs (11)	81
Lee Andre Aglae (11)	82
Ronnie Charles David Higgs (11)	82
Holly Venton (12)	83
Ryan Johnson (13)	83
Stacey Marie Tonks (13)	84
Rhys Floyde (13)	84
Melissa Watts	85
Emily Lewin (12)	85
Amy White (12)	86
Grace Caitlin Donnelly (11)	86
Aidan Pearce (13)	87
Ellie Adams (14)	87
Midnight Millett-Bangs (11)	88
Joseph Mauceri (13)	88
Patsi Weedon (13)	89
Sam Fisk (11)	89
Tanya Eastwood (11)	89
Lauren Jessica Froste (11)	90

St Mary's School, Colchester

Alice Neil (11)	90
Jess Francis (14)	91
Jessica Hale (11)	92
Eleanor Jolliffe (13)	93
Coco Boyd Ratcliffe (12)	94
Helen Pannell (15)	95
Maddie Sims (14)	96
Ellen Gage (15)	96
Libby Mead (12)	97
Rebecca Ennion (14)	97
Joanne Illidge (13)	98
Bryony Fenn (13)	99

The Alec Hunter Humanities College

Reece Squire (14)	100
Ivan Shipulin (14)	101
Ekenna Oji (14)	102
Christine Nelson (13)	103

Martyn Richardson (12)	103
Hope Dodge (11)	104
Laura Wiffen (14)	104
Emily Bunyan (11)	105

The Boswells School

Rhiannon Garrard (12)	105

The Sweyne Park School

Hollie Robinson (14)	106
Daniel Waggon (13)	107
Andrew Dartnell (12)	107
Jason Keys (13)	108
Daniel Moore (11)	108
Kai McKechnie (12)	109
Aaron Jones (11)	109
Olivia Unwin (11)	110
Freddie Bentley (12)	110
Michael Bewers (11)	111
Bradley Keys (12)	111
Jessica Sterling (13)	112
Rachel Hudson (16)	112
Alice Hodkinson (15)	113
Harry Ludlow (15)	113
George Barker (13)	114
Connor Thompson (12)	114
Gemma Gilson (12)	115
Shauna Quinn (11)	115
Megan Leighton (13)	115
Charlotte Mayo (11)	116
David Greenslade (12)	116
George Izod (11)	116
Georgina Davis (11)	117
Mitchell Lambe (12)	117

Thurstable School

Jessica Rowe (13)	117
Charlotte Hood (12)	118
Toby Price (12)	119
Megan House (12)	120
Rachel Etherington (14)	121
Elliot Hawkins (12)	122
Sonny Trigg (13)	123
Rebecca Lockwood (13)	124
Amy Dignum (11)	124
Heather Acketts (12)	125

Jodie Haertel (11)	125
Heidi Sale (12)	126
Elizabeth David (13)	126
Katie Smart (13)	127
Callum Hultquist (13)	127
Jamie David Allen (13)	128
Charley Bowhill (12)	128
Billy Martyn (11)	129
Charlie Flanagan(11)	129
Mary-Ann Anthony (13)	130
Kelsey Graham (11)	130
William Pryke (13)	131
Kester Reeve (11)	131
Ellie-Jane Oliver (12)	132
Charlotte Leavett-Shove (11)	132
Joss Saunders (12)	133
Katie Wollington (11)	133
Georgia Kyne (12)	134
Ellen Trollope (11)	134
Charleigh Green (12)	135
Gemma Bird (13)	135
Katy Rose Payne (11)	136
Robert James Gill (13)	136
Daisy Smith (13)	137
Emme Ross (13)	137
Lucy Greed (11)	138
Samuel James (11)	138
Sonya Zemmiri (11)	139
James Johnson (11)	139
Molly-Rose Gosling (13)	140
Mark Oldham (12)	140
Lewis Scrivener (14)	141
Thomas Dale (11)	141
Charlotte Smith (13)	142
Katie Polley (12)	142
Madeleine Nixson (12)	143
Dolly Trigg (11)	143
Hannah Whyburd (12)	144
Bethany Dickinson (13)	144
Suzanne Howes (15)	145
David Owers (11)	145
Jessica Vant (13)	146
Harriet Tsoi (13)	146
Ellen Blacow (13)	147
Natasha Shade (13)	147
Thomas Bellotti (12)	148
Molly Munson (11)	148
Sam Griffin (13)	149
Jake Monk (11)	149
Lewis Johnson (12)	150
Jasmine Everett (11)	150
Cora Arrowsmith (13)	151
Kirby Taylor (11)	151
Shawn Cornish (13)	152
Matthew Khan (11)	152
Maria-Ellen Carslake (11)	153
Hannah Kane (13)	153
Katherine Read (13)	154
Bertie Rigby (12)	154
Kristie Smith (13)	155
Jamie Peachey (12)	155
Thomas Crossley (11)	156
Pele Heydon (13)	156
Michaela Richer (11)	157
Joshua French (11)	157
Peter Greenwood (12)	158
Emily Lane (13)	158
Maddison Seaber (14)	158
James Culley (13)	159
William Weller (13)	159
Charlie Hammond(13)	159
Amy Georgina Lee Begg (11)	160
Luke Gregory Towers (13)	160
Emma Dyer (12)	160
Luke James (11)	161
Evangeline Perry (13)	161
Oliver Mills (12)	162

The Poems

The Ice Wolf

High in the Arctic north, a land all covered in snow,
The ice wolf hunts unseen, unheard while the wailing north winds blow,
Caribou from a wandering herd,
Graze peacefully on the tundra,
The lone wolf stalks around the scrub,
His claws dig keenly under.

Not far away a tribe prepares for dusk,
It's to tend the livestock,
Before predators arouse,
Oblivious to the rising danger,
The herder takes his time.

Meanwhile the hunter has spotted easy prey,
A tender faun skipping away from safety,
He drops silently, slowly,
Muscles tensed, he crawls forward,
So close he could . . .
A jingle of bells catches his attention
The herder has arrived,
The faun gallops back to the herd, happy, unknowing.

The wolf melts into the background,
Starving, sullen and outwitted,
They would never know how close he'd come,
Until they heard,
A sound feared by even the great whales,
The blood-curdling howl of the ice wolf.

Lea Wood (12)
Anglo European School

You're The Greatest

When your best friends turn against you
You cry so much you cannot do
And the tears just come down your face
You cannot find a right place
Don't be offended by stupid words
You can do whatever your heart tells you
'Cause you're beautiful inside
And it doesn't matter how you look from outside
When your heart cannot go any longer
You don't feel any stronger
And you feel so tired but you cannot sleep
It's time for you to take a grip
Don't be offended by stupid words
You can do whatever your heart tells you
'Cause you're beautiful inside
And it doesn't matter how you look from outside
And when you feel it's time to die
Don't worry, it's just a lie
Look inside yourself and see a stronger person you can be
So don't be scared of them, you are the greatest
You can do whatever you want
They are the fakest!

Aleyna Costin (11)
Anglo European School

The Rise And Fall Of Yeast Products

Before yeast, did we not have lesser expectations?
If all was flat, did we not notice those who fell behind?
Those who were unable to rise and didn't quite make the final production line?
Was there no competition, as all were dough and dough the same,
No high and mighty, haughty ways, none rejected, none subject to a special glaze?
Before yeast, would we all have made the batch?
Would none be rendered redundant, when the time came to dispatch?

Amy Morgan (17)
Anglo European School

– Essex

Waters Blue

Deep in the waters blue,
Whales sing their songs to you,
Their voices may be deafening,
But some humans are too.

Where the waves wash up stones,
A fish may be far from home,
Although a sight in aquariums,
Their families feel all alone.

Somewhere, nowhere near the shore,
Being a castaway would be a downright bore.
Starfish lie in the middle of nowhere,
Wanting to rest some more.

When some sails go out to sea,
There's an adventure for you and me.
For the seaside is full of surprises,
This is what makes it a wonderful place to be.

Near where the shells are in heaps,
You could sit for hours hearing all sounds,
Mermaids singing lullabies to last for eternity,
This is why I love the sea.

Maisie Allen (12)
Anglo European School

Different

Being different is not a bad thing
Some black, some white, some fat and thin
People will laugh, make comments too
But being insecure is not the best thing to do.

People will judge by what they see
Ha, ha, they say and smile with glee
But don't worry, they're just a bully.

Jessica Green (12)
Anglo European School

Teenage Life
(Dedicated to Scarlett Clark)

Now that you have turned 16,
I am sure that you are keen,
To find out about the dos and don'ts.
I don't want to hear any whinges or moans,
I know that you don't want any responsibilities
And you don't want to have any maturity,
But to every piece of negativity,
There comes a bit of positivity.
You will start to grow out of your high-pitched voice
And you suddenly won't care about your poise.
But hey, don't worry, you can still sing in the shower,
Dance to Britney in your room,
Don't be afraid to shout out 'girl power',
Still using your high-pitched voice.
Obviously you will start scoring boys,
Surely that must be the best bit?
You will start clubbing with your girls
And if you are lucky, have your first date.
You could say teenage life is extreme,
To wrap it all up I will just say, it's a scream!

Tobias Clark (14)
Anglo European School

Animal Cruelty

Animal cruelty must be a faulty
Bears' coats shouldn't be shaved
All these guys are really naughty
Killing elephants for their tusks
Stopping this practice is a must.

Lions and tigers it must be said
Should be roaming and not be dead
Polar bears are dying because of global warming
If we don't do something, nothing will be forming

Animal cruelty must be a faulty.

Tamarra Atkinson (11)
Anglo European School

Crash

Faster and faster the car is going,
The police chasing those idiots, what are they doing?
Martin shouted, 'Stop this car!'
But Apache didn't listen to what Martin was saying.

As they approached Green Street,
They came to a junction,
The lights were red, but Pete said, 'Go for it!'
They were hit by a van and they rolled twice.

The ambulance comes, followed by the fire engine,
Mark was pulled out but Martin wasn't!
Mark cried out, 'That's my mate in there!'
And then there was a huge explosion . . .

Neville Firattan (12)
Anglo European School

The Crash

Smash! There goes the windscreen.
Boom! No, not the engine!
Sizzle! Up roar the flames.
Why does it have to be me?

Silence, you can only hear sirens,
How could I be tricked into this?
Frightened and unconscious,
Terrified and tearful.

Why me? Why me? Why me?
Now I'm scarred and disabled.

Conrad Stace (12)
Anglo European School

Being Different
To be different is a horrible thing
Bullies telling you horrible things
You like different music, style and taste
You hate being judged by your face
You feel unconfident, you feel insecure
But it's your choice for feeling that way
Not everyone can be the same.

Olukorede Banjo (12)
Anglo European School

Schooldays
I woke up in the morning
I saw the sun shining
I went down the stairs
And I saw my mum smiling.

Breakfast on the table
Got dropped at school
In my dad's flashy car
Looking very cool.

See my friends talking
Talking very loud
See them all smiling
Looking very proud.

The bell then just rang
Everyone was in class
Staring out of the window
Waiting for home time.

Home time had come
The children started to run
Running towards home
Before my mum started to moan.

Aniqa Riba & Kajal Dhingra (11)
Barking Abbey Comprehensive Upper School

Lies That Go Too Far

My silly cousin Fran tells the teachers lies.
It goes so far they almost cry.

This is a story about one time
According to the teacher Fran did a crime.

One rainy day in the room of art
My silly cousin Fran claimed the teacher did a fart.

'Stop telling lies,' the teacher said to Fran
But according to her the fun had just began . . .

Fran embarrassed him, joked about him, made him cry
She made him feel hurt and also very shy.

All at once when the teacher was really mad
He boomed, 'Go to the head, so he can call your dad!'

Fran started walking off to the head
She started to think, it could be funny instead.

When she got there, she swung open the door
There was the head, her dad and one more . . .

There was her mum for the first time in nine
This time she knew she'd be home with a broken spine

Fran thought fast, she faked to faint
Her mum got her up and smacked her like paint.

On their way home her mum had to say
Fran was suspended for more than a day . . .

Lybah Kiran (11)
Barking Abbey Comprehensive Upper School

I Dream . . .

I dream of a place,
Where people can be understood.
I dream of a place,
Where I don't get misunderstood.
I dream of a place,
Where people don't need to be told anymore.
I dream of a place,
Where there is no war.
I dream of a place,
Where people can be friends.
I dream of a place,
Where people can make amends.
I dream of a place,
Where I'm filled with joy.
I dream of a place,
Where there is no bad boy.
I dream of a place,
Where we can all dream
I dream of a place,
Where people don't scream.
I dream of a place,
Where clouds are as soft as candyfloss.
I dream of a place,
Where stars are bright,
That roam the night.
I dream . . .

Whitney Goold-Walters (11)
Barking Abbey Comprehensive Upper School

I Wanna Go Home

I wanna go home, I wanna go home,
To the place where I belong,
The place where I feel safe from harm.

Why did it happen to me?
Where am I?
Where is my food, bone and bed?
I just wanna go home!

I wanna go home, I wanna go home,
My bruises and scratches are sore,
And I feel like I'm gonna die,
I'm cold and wet,
Muddy and dirty,
I'm lost!
I just wanna go home!

Why did it happen to me?
Where am I?
Where's my food, bone and bed?
I just want to go home, where I belong.
I just want to go and find my family.
I just wanna go home!

Megan McDermott (12)
Barking Abbey Comprehensive Upper School

War

War is the place not to be,
War you don't want to see,
The sound of guns everywhere,
Flying through the air.
The sound of screams and cries makes me shiver,
As these people are too young to wither.
Can't anyone just see what the soldiers are going through?
No, you just don't have a clue.
The war makes me cry, seeing innocent people die.
At least they are in Heaven now, not harmed anymore,
Resting in peace, no longer at war.

Maisie Crowley (12)
Barking Abbey Comprehensive Upper School

The Darkness Of Pain

Blood pouring out, scarlet as a petal of a rose.
Nothing can wash it away, including the power of a jet hose.
Lying there, as still as a lifeless dummy,
There would never be humour, nothing could be funny.

The force of the heavy wind blowing my wavy hair,
The key emotion was hatred and despair.
Would there ever be love and affection, would anyone care?
All I could see were trickles of crystal clear tears.

I glared up into the dark night sky,
Wanting to leave this horrific nightmare and silently fly,
Without hearing another bullet fired,
I just wanted back the old, magnificent world I admired.

I began to shudder then peacefully slept till dawn,
When I then saw horror-stricken folks mourn.
Could I escape, could I ever flee?
Did this bolt of pain hit all, or unfortunately just me?

Manisha Juttla (12)
Barking Abbey Comprehensive Upper School

Schooldays

It's the first day of school,
New teachers and children,
New everything.
The bell has just rung,
There is a big pile of people everywhere,
Pushing and shoving all over the place.
The school is so big and there are so many people.
In lesson the teachers tell me not to be so quiet and look so worried,
But I'm just shy.
The best part of school is my friends.
We will be friends until the end.
I see them every day at school,
They are fun and cool.
I like my secondary school but it will take some getting used to,
'Cause primary school is over, but learning never ends.

Ellie Rouse (11)
Barking Abbey Comprehensive Upper School

Courage And Bravery
(Based on wrestling)

Walking along the walkway strong and proud
The crowd shouts out your name long and loud
Mind quickly working what the result will be
Will it involve bruises all over your knee?
Your opponent looks at you with a mysterious glare
Already you know this will be a nightmare
Legs trembling, heart racing
As you stare at the one you are facing
Thinking of the pain you can't bear it
As you try to look brave and tremendously fit
The match starts as the opposing throw punches
You notice the crowd cheering in bunches
Now it's your chance, the opening is clear
You finally know you have faced your fear
You exit the ring screaming inside you
As a set of crowd continually boo.

Karan Singh Ahir (11)
Barking Abbey Comprehensive Upper School

Alone

When I'm all broken down,
I need a place to run to.
Can't figure out,
I'm so lost and all alone.
And my head is tired,
I need a place to scream in,
I'm really lost.
Alone in the dark corners of the room,
Can't think of anything to do,
Fear runs down my throat,
I'm alone.
Then comes the light,
Which is ever so bright,
To show me the way,
Which is to make friends.

Sabiha Rahman Chowdhury (12)
Barking Abbey Comprehensive Upper School

Animal Animals

The dog was fat,
Sitting on a hat,
The cat was small,
Eating near the pool,
The donkey was a fool,
Playing with a tool,
The tiger was roaring,
The sky was falling,
The ant was tiny,
The gold was shiny,
The fish was smelly,
The people eating jelly,
The crocodile was green,
The bullies were mean,
The fly was buzzing like a bee,
Which was very hard to see,
Towards the apple tree.

Rahid Ahmed (12)
Barking Abbey Comprehensive Upper School

Happy Tears

Happy tears were back then,
When we laughed and smiled at each other.
But then, *she* came along,
Where she didn't belong
And that's where the tears started
And the fears the people, made them so worried.
How the people would cry,
As the sly girl fooled them.
One day she was not to be seen,
Where has she been? And where is she now?
As the people would gather around,
We knew this was the end of her.
How everyone felt sorry but happy on the inside!
That was when the happy tears came back.

Hadisa Rehman (11)
Barking Abbey Comprehensive Upper School

A British Muslim

A British Muslim
A wonder of life
I love the great Him
I don't carry a knife
I love my mum
I love her to bits
I'm not that dumb
I love studying the Blitz!
I love my dad
I'm not that bad
I'm not always sad
But I might be mad
Man U is the best
My cousin's from the west
I visit him every day
In the month of May!

Hashim Mahmood (12)
Barking Abbey Comprehensive Upper School

Stabbing Is Bad

My friend got stabbed
My emotion got grabbed
My mum said it would be OK
My voice said go away
My dad gave me a smile
My face dropped a mile
My friend's funeral came
My sister said what a shame
My friend's life was over
My thought was to live it over
My present was a bat to him
I wish it could be better
I am writing it in a letter
To let my emotions out.

Harry Murphy (11)
Barking Abbey Comprehensive Upper School

Friends

Friends go to the ends of the Earth,
That is definitely worth it,
Some friends are friends from birth,
Most friends stay for a bit.

The friend trap includes a fake friend,
They don't stay there until the end,
A fake friend is worth nothing,
Don't fall into the trap.

Some friends have instant quarrels,
But you can fix it with a sorry,
Then everything is back to normal,
Until next time . . .

Shivani Rajput (11)
Barking Abbey Comprehensive Upper School

She Thinks

She thinks she's the best
But she'll never win a test
She thinks she's all it
But she'll never learn how to sit
She thinks she's going to win
But she'll never use a pin
She thinks she has a good sight
But she'll never have a good night's sleep
She thinks she's a princess
But she'll never find her prince
She thinks she has good knees
But she'll never have a cup of tea.

Adiba Begum
Barking Abbey Comprehensive Upper School

The Jungle Cry

If I were a tiger and you were the jungle,
Imagine how much I would spend with thee,
With the rustle of your leaves you would whisper to me,
Everything was perfect with me and thee.
However, then came something,
The *humans* that were after me,
They cut your leaves and flowers as you protected me,
Bit by bit you started to disappear.
Then the only thing that mattered to me was gone,
Trapped in this land alone, without my favourite, thee.
Waiting for time to pass me by and trying to hope that thee
Didn't do what he did just for the love of me.

Amy Stainsbury (11)
Barking Abbey Comprehensive Upper School

Animals

Why do we eat pigs?
Why do we wear such wigs?
Why do we kill whales?
Why, why do we need it now?
Why do we hunt animals?
Tell me now or I'll do a cannonball.
Why do we do such things?
Why now are you pulling my strings?
Animals, animals everywhere,
But are they treated with love and care?
Why are they killed here?
Why not till next year?

Lemmar Reid (11)
Barking Abbey Comprehensive Upper School

What I Did Yesterday

Yesterday I cleaned my room
But my sister took my broom.

I didn't really like her much
But then she started speaking Dutch.

My sister made noise
And took my toys.

I like to sleep
By counting sheep.

My sister is 10
And so is my friend.

Tehseen Ahmad (11)
Barking Abbey Comprehensive Upper School

Media Says

The media says our generation is lethal,
They focus on us and not other people,
The media says, '17, 18, 19, oh they're a pain!'
I've heard enough, the media is insane!
The media says, 'Stabbing, killing, it's the teens.'
Stereotype their way through life, no facts, all fiction.
Now we speak as a favour to ourselves
And we say, 'We all are youth, not all bad,
You focus on the sour but not the sweet.'

After that . . .
Media says nothing.

Karim Benotmane (11)
Barking Abbey Comprehensive Upper School

If I Were . . .

If I were a tiger, would that mean I was fierce?
If I were a bird, would that mean I was free?
If I were a snail, would that make me slow?
If I were a fish, would that make me a good swimmer?
If I were an elephant, would that make me big?
If I were a cheetah, would that make me fast?
If I were a mouse, would that make me small?
If I were a giraffe, would that make me tall?
If I were a hyena, would that mean I had a great sense of humour?

Luckvir Bhati
Barking Abbey Comprehensive Upper School

Wasn't Me

Drugs and crimes are on the news but who will pay?
Me or you?
Who really is to blame?
Who really makes the knives and drugs?
So why do teenagers get the blame?
People die every second
And some die at a young age
But who's the killer?
Me or you?

Shibaz Hussain
Barking Abbey Comprehensive Upper School

Life

Walking through the woods, crunching on the leaves,
Thinking how they fall off,
Listening to the animals talk to each other,
Wondering if they actually understand one another.
Other students, walking past saying,
'I don't understand animals, well at least we have a life.'
Sometimes other things apart from humans,
Look like they have no life, but they do, like us.

Jannat Rashad (11)
Barking Abbey Comprehensive Upper School

World War II

All the men that have been through so much pain,
Have now got some time to hopefully regain,
Through all the devastation,
Have made sensation,
They have made us proud,
For making themselves so loud,
They put themselves through a lot
And some have been shot,
But we are ever so proud to call them our men.

Zoe Chafer (11)
Barking Abbey Comprehensive Upper School

Untitled

I live through my dark existence,
Only to bask in your beauty,
Your eyes that shine like sapphires,
Your smile that brightens even my sad existence.

I long to touch you,
To hold you in my arms, but I cannot,
For your heart belongs to another,
So I can only love you from afar.

I never knew there could be a better tomorrow,
But you've come into my life and taken away all my sorrow.
My days of sadness are a thing of the past,
Because I have found the love at last.

My days of emptiness are gone for good,
Because you have filled a void in my heart that you should
You've opened a window,
You've shown me the light,
And my love for you
Will continue to burn bright.

Abbie Kinerman (14)
Chase High School

Teaching Him A Lesson!

If I told you the truth
What would you do?
If I asked you who you love
Would you say you?
I cried on your shoulder
And you turned your head
Did you think of my feelings?
Yes, I heard what you said!

Don't tell me you can explain
I've heard it all before
You say one more chance
But I don't want you anymore
Well, I suppose this is your karma
Players get what they deserve
Your kisses weren't so sweet
Oops, did I touch a nerve?

I guess now I'm not so easy
I didn't just jump into bed
Because us Essex girls were known for that
But honey, I'm one step ahead
I bet you thought I was on my knees
But girls with pride don't beg
You were just a waste of time
You left my heart cracking like an egg.

I'm not like all your other birds
I don't follow your every demand
It's about time you realised
You're under my command
You no longer have the power
You no longer hold my heart
Because I now know what love is
I guess someone else is playing your part!

Emma Turner
Chase High School

My Poem

Children with no home,
Thinking they're all alone,
Suffering, violence, famine,
Does anyone care about them?

Abuse and name calling,
Kids outside brawling,
Poverty everywhere,
Nobody seems to care.

Infuriated parents,
Causing lots of arguments,
As their kids stealing,
More find it appealing.

Tortured at school,
They're more vulnerable,
As they get a bad education,
They're affected later on.

All these things are an issue,
As you hear on the news,
The teenagers and kids are blamed,
But are the adults just ashamed?

So, what's the cause of this madness?
Kids hatred from their parents,
Maybe alcohol or cannabis,
Are the ones influencing this.

Michael Berry (14)
Chase High School

A Blast Of Colour

Orange fumes drop from the sky,
The colour bursts and always flies,
The darkness I do not fear,
As I do not drip a tear,
A blast of colour comes from the sky,
I lay down my head and ask why.

Charlotte Tanner (11)
Chase High School

Who's That Girl?

You see that girl, sitting with all the bullies,
Watch as she turns her head looking for her prey,
You can feel the tension in her eyes,
Picking on people because they look different,
Even though she's not perfect herself.

You see that girl, squashed in the corner,
Look as she lowers her head as the laughter revolves around her,
Seeing everyone look down at her as though she's non-existent,
Wishing the day would hurry up and pass by,
Even though she's just a human like everyone else.

You see that girl, sitting by herself in the library,
Wondering why she couldn't look like everyone else,
Self-harming, depression and pain,
All passing through every minute of every day,
Even though she still tries to attach a smile to her face.

You see that girl, brushing her hair in the mirror,
Thinking that she's more important than the others,
Deep down she knows that she's equal to everyone else,
But she has a dark, hidden secret inside that she just can't express,
Even though she looks brave, deep down she's unwanted.

You see the girls around me,
All wanting to express themselves,
But there's one thing that's stopping them from doing that,
They need love, care and attention.

Abbie MacGavin (14)
Chase High School

The Fly

A crack, a creepy cavern
A piece of Blu-Tack like a giant sticky heaven
A drop of ink like a sea of black
A spider web, a gigantic trap.

Cameron Russell (12)
Chase High School

Rumours

I once heard if you loved somebody you'd hear them out,
Before believing everyone else and moping about.
But you heard the rumours and you believed those lies,
I thought you were different from the other guys.

Just stop for a sec and think through the facts;
Rumours are rumours, and we're stronger than that.
Those entire lies, they were plainly not true!
Believe me when I say: 'I love you.'

In class when you stare, I feel the room get colder,
Whilst I remember cuddling up to your amiable shoulder.
I don't want this to end, if I had my way,
Together, you and I, that's how we'd stay.

From now on I'll lock up my heart and the key I'll throw,
I'll fake a smile with every 'hello'.
Just you assume that I'm fine and it's not affecting me,
But I'm throbbing inside, why can't you see?

Charlie Ward
Chase High School

I Was Bullied

I was bullied
I was bullied for the way I look
I was bullied for the way I act
I was bullied for having no friends
I had no friends.

I was bullied
I was bullied for being new
I was bullied for being clever
I was bullied for looking weird
I didn't look weird.

I hated school
So I never went
Because, I was bullied . . .

Joe Lawrence (14)
Chase High School

Untitled

What shall I do about the bullies?
They're truly getting to me.
All their mocking and taunting,
To face them is daunting.

I lie alone at night
Wondering why I deserved this.
As I take blows and punches to the head,
I think to myself, *why this?*
When I could be lying peacefully in a deathbed.

Lying awake in my bed,
Monday's tomorrow.
I'm not going back to that place of dread.

I guess it's time . . .
I pick up a knife,
Jab myself forcefully and end my life . . .

Jay Duncumb (14)
Chase High School

Magic

Do you know what magic is?
It may not be what you think.
It's not some silly potions that make you shrink,
It's not a witch in a big purple hat
That eats you up and that's why now she's fat.
Now listen carefully, I'll tell you what it is,
Are you listening with your ears?
Magic is something that you can't see,
It's surrounding all of us, you and me.
Love is magic, did you know that?
You can't disagree and that's a fact!
Now you know what magic is,
I hope you didn't miss any of this.

Julia Cichocka (11)
Chase High School

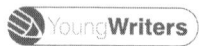

Untitled

I want to be the same
Who am I to blame?
Life is hard but I get on
My parents try to help
But I just want to be the same
Who am I to blame?

I want to be the same
Who am I to blame?
All the kids laugh and joke
They find excuses to prod and poke
I want to be the same
Who am I to blame?

Robert Elliott
Chase High School

Bullying

Bullies can ruin your life,
With words, or with a knife
Because of what I did,
I was bullied as a kid,
It made me hate school,
I was never very cool,
People treated me as if I was a fool,
Bullies pick on people who they think are nerds,
To win my battles I use words,
I admit I was a geek at school,
But now I am rich,
So now who's the fool?

Dominic Glatter (14)
Chase High School

Fear

Fear is all around me,
It's running through my head,
It never ever leaves me alone,
Even when I'm in bed.
It tries to frighten me,
It tries to scare me,
It does its best to hurt me,
Oh yes, I can see,
I wish I could get away from this fear,
This fear is killing me,
Oh yes, it is!

Sarah Weaver (11)
Chase High School

Happy Hallowe'en

Here comes Hallowe'en
With ghosts and ghouls
If you don't have candy
You'll look like fools

Don't go to bed
Because you'll have pictures in your head
Of the ghosts and ghouls dancing
Like big, fat fools
Here comes Hallowe'en
So don't be fools.

Daniella Hare (11)
Chase High School

Animal - Haiku

Across the blue sky
An albatross flies calmly
Looking for its tea.

Alexander De Boick (11)
Chase High School

Juliet's Desperate Plea

Oh Romeo, Romeo take me away
Take me away from all this pain
All I'm after is just a simple piece of laughter
But instead we've just struck disaster
Oh, let's run away
It's our fate
It's our destiny
Oh why won't you run away with me?
I am making a drastic plea
Please run away with me.

Bertha Sibanda (11)
Chase High School

My Best Friend: Sabena Khanom

You're my best friend and that is true
Never forget that because I love you.
We went through moments which we loved
From good to sad and happy to bad.
There are many things that I love about you
You mean the world to me
And you will always be in my heart
Even if we're miles apart.
She is like an owl, both beautiful and wise
She is like a ghost whose spirit never dies!

Sajada Rahman (11)
Chase High School

I'm The Boy

I'm the boy on his own in the playground.
I'm the boy that nobody talks to.
I'm the boy that everyone hates.
I'm the one that everyone uses as a punch bag.
I'm the boy that sits in his room crying all night.
I'm the boy that gets bullied every day.
I'm the boy you look at in disgust.
I'm the boy who's crying out for a friend.
I'm the boy whose mum found him with a rope around his neck.

Josh Hindle (14)
Chase High School

Socks

Socks can be smelly
Socks can be nice
But whoever said that these socks
Are not bright?

These socks are special
These socks are clever
So keep it a secret
Forever and ever!

Paige Elcoate (11)
Chase High School

Mountains

Big,
Snowy, massive,
Gigantic, fantastic, beautiful,
Creepy, empty,
Cold,
Rocky, sloping,
Mountainous, incredible, volcanic,
Snow-capped, stormy,
Tall.

Terry Higgins (15)
Children's Support Service

Anorexia

When she looks in the mirror,
She's disgusted at what she sees.
Only she can imagine
What she wants to be.

Hungry she is feeling,
But the fat prevents her from eating.
Mentally and physically punishing herself
For as long as her heart is beating.

Her angular shape,
All skin and bones,
Makes her body cry out,
But she never moans.

Pretty she wants to be,
But rounded she will always feel,
Help is what she needs,
Constantly told she is mentally ill.

Smaller she gets
And shrinking day by day,
But the picture she sees in her eyes,
Tells her it's never going to go away.

Havannah Withey (15)
Children's Support Service

Pearl Harbour

Death
  Terror
    Disaster
      Catastrophe
        Abomination
      Kamikaze
    Killing
  Blood
    Fighting
      Fire
        Planes
          Fear
        Blasts
        Explosions

War!

Daniel Hill (15)
Children's Support Service

Peace

Love
Freedom
Happiness
Considerate
Negotiation
Pacification
Serenity
Victory
Goodwill
Faith
Doves.

Alfie Lawrence (15)
Children's Support Service

Sadness

Sadness.
It's a grey blanket.
It hangs from your soul.
Sadness.
It's the Grim Reaper.
It's the cold winter air.
It's the person who spoils everything.
It can be a crazed mare.
Sadness.
It grips your heart in an iron coffin.
It makes a stone in your throat.
Can you make a sadness antidote?
Sadness.
It makes you weak.
It's an overpowering force that is also sleek.
How? How can such a powerful force be invisible?
Sadness.
You lose your favourite pet.
'He's gone to a better place,' the adults say.
Nowhere near a better place than in my arms!
Happens when you lose someone,
Someone you love.
Grief then runs as if it's blood through the family.
It catches through the family like the flu.
Not just dying,
It's a best mate moving away,
It's your first love dumping you,
It's Mum and Dad arguing,
It's something you've lost,
It's someone leaving you.

Hannah Clarke (12)
Clacton County High School

I'm Not That Kind Of Person

Please do not label me, no not at all,
I'm not that kind of person, who will let
You stand and watch me fall.

I change every day, into who I want to be,
I'm not that kind of person, who will let
You label me.

I am like a book, sometimes easy to read
But hard to understand.
I'm not that kind of person, to be included in a brand.

Populars, scenes, emos and geeks,
But I'm not that kind of person, to be
Placed as one of these.

Because I am me, a unique person,
Not a category, nor a label.

My emotions are mixed, my head is held high,
Because I'm not that kind of person,
To sit there and cry.

I am me. The person who is different,
Who changes every day.
You can't label me, because you will
Never find the *same* me!

Molly Blake (12)
Clacton County High School

Why?

Why must you always humiliate me?
Why must you tease and torment, like I'm not a human being?
Why must you point at me and gasp like I'm an animal at the zoo?
Why must you spread rumours about me that are hurtful and untrue?
Why do you hate me so?

I know I'm weird, I know I'm strange,
At the end of the day, we're all the same,
Because you know the words are untrue,
You wouldn't like it if they were said about you.

Why must you turn everyone against me?
Why can't you just leave me be?
Why must everything I touch leave me?
Why must life be a cruel reality?
Why do you hate me so?

But I do have the courage to stand up to you,
Because I can tell someone the honest truth
And after a while it does get lame,
So please give it up, we're all the same.

Don't bully me please, it's no fun game,
Don't hurt me or anyone else ever again.

Amber Bellinger (12)
Clacton County High School

Emo-Tional

'Look, she's emo, can't you see her scars?'
'Maybe it's 'cause all day I just hear your laughs.'
Who are you to judge me?
To tell me what to be?
Never judge a book by its cover until you get to read.

There are scars on the outside, but your words cut deeper,
But you don't control me, I am my keeper.
Look what you've done to yourself and then me,
You're teasing me for being who I want to be.

I'm sure there are fault in everyone here
I don't need to point out people's weak points,
I don't need to live in fear.

Overall the bigger person is me,
Because I will forever be who I want to be,
Not changed by anyone, especially not you,
Because I may be stronger, yes,
Stronger than you.

Siobhan Tillyer (12)
Clacton County High School

I Just Want To Go Home

Why do I have to be here
And live with this fear?
I want to be alone,
I want to go home.

I could be playing in the park,
From morning to dark,
Sleep all through the day
And wake to the sun rays.

Today's been so bad,
Making me so sad,
I wish I was having fun,
With a smile as bright as the sun.

C J Mayes (12)
King Edward VI Grammar School

School Life

School life . . . what can be said?
Apart from lunch, where you can buy garlic bread,
It's mostly our head buried in the text,
Always moaning and always perplexed . . .
However, you put aside the bad sides,
And you will see that the teachers and the work are our guides
And help us in our strides,
To help us understand the world outside.
Yes, they might be strict,
And yes, they might start a huge conflict,
But for every negative,
There is a positive.
For there are teachers who are not so penetrative,
But nice, helpful and make you believe
That school's not such a bad place,
To extend your mind to a reasonable case.

Mainak Datta (13)
King Edward VI Grammar School

A Twisted Talent

Everyone has a talent in them,
For inside there is a precious gem,
But one is there who doesn't show,
Hidden secrets, nobody knows.
Everybody's special in their own way,
Some are just gifted, no words to say.
It's just me, warped and twisted,
With so many talents in my mind,
It's just so bewildering to find.
Sports, arts, people, show with passion,
Out in the world, others have their fashion.
But for me, too compact to cast on . . .
Different things - fling when I was born.
In my heart, there is a big fortune,
To bust it out - in the right opportune!
I'm still here - warped and twisted . . .

Kurian George (12)
King Edward VI Grammar School

I Am A Teenager

I am a teenager, growing by the day,
I am a teenager, with zits and armpit spray.

I'm an adolescent, rebellious and immature,
I'm an adolescent, well is there a cure?

I am a student, homework? *No way!*
I am a student, could be doing stuff today.

I am a teenager, it could be worse,
I am a teenager, I could be an oldie in a hearse.

I'm an adolescent, approaching adulthood,
I'm an adolescent, get a good job I should.

I am a student, exams coming up,
I am a student, gonna go right to the top!

James Beaumont (12)
King Edward VI Grammar School

Sounds Of The World

The tiniest sound in the world
Must be the Earth revolving slowly.

The spookiest sound in the world
Must be a scorpion walking up my window.

The noisiest sound in the world
Must be a dinosaur stomping through the jungle.

The happiest sound in the world
Must be a dolphin diving and jumping in the sea.

Aaron Holness (11)
Kingswode Hoe School

Sounds

The tiniest sound in the world
Must be my dog clicking his paws on the carpet.

The spookiest sound in the world
Must be the thunder clouds crashing in the night-time sky.

The noisiest sound in the world
Must be Mum calling like an elephant marching.

The happiest sound in the world
Must be music I listen to on my iPod.

Ellie Longman (11)
Kingswode Hoe School

Sounds

The tiniest sound in the world
Must be a rat scattering.

The spookiest sound in the world
Must be a snake slithering.

The noisiest sound in the world
Must be a dog barking in the middle of the night.

The happiest sound in the world
Must be birds singing in the morning.

Bailey Saunders (11)
Kingswode Hoe School

Sounds

The tiniest sound in the world
Must be a butterfly flying in the sky.

The spookiest sound in the world
Must be a witch cackling in the sky.

The noisiest sound in the world
Must be dogs woofing and barking for their tea.

The happiest sound in the world
Must be a fish swimming in the sea.

Jessica Blake (11)
Kingswode Hoe School

Sounds

The tiniest sound in the world
Must be the pen lid clicking onto the pen.

The spookiest sound in the world
Must be a ghost making me jump.

The noisiest sound in the world
My dogs barking for their dinner.

The happiest sound in the world
Must be mummy talking to me.

Caleb Baccarini (11)
Kingswode Hoe School

Sounds

The tiniest sound in the world
Must be birds tweeting in the tree.

The spookiest sound in the world
Must be thunder and lightning that frightens me.

The noisiest sound in the world
Must be a car zooming down the road at me.

The happiest sound in the world
Must be a horse clip-clopping on the street.

Corey Byrne (11)
Kingswode Hoe School

Sounds In The World

The tiniest sound in the world
Must be a clock tick-tocking in my ear beside me.

The spookiest sound in the world
Must be a witch cackling nastily.

The noisiest sound in the world
Must be an elephant stomping in the jungle safari.

The happiest sound in the world
Must be a guinea pig squeaking merrily to me.

Jodie Lawrence (11)
Kingswode Hoe School

Sounds

The tiniest sound in the world
Must be guinea pigs nibbling cabbage for tea.

The spookiest sound in the world
Must be a bat flapping its wings at me.

The noisiest sound in the world
Must be a volcano erupting, spurting lava.

The happiest sound in the world
Must be rabbits jumping over the trampoline.

Jake Candler (11)
Kingswode Hoe School

Sounds

The tiniest sound in the world
Must be a mouse tiptoeing in the house.

The spookiest sound in the world
Must be the bell dinging and donging.

The noisiest sound in the world
Must be cats calling, crying for me.

The happiest sound in the world
Must be my mum and dad and Gemma telling funny jokes.

Emma Rawling (11)
Kingswode Hoe School

The Sounds

The tiniest sound in the world
Must be an ant crawling along a leaf.

The spookiest sound in the world
Must be a ghost.

The noisiest sound in the world
Must be chairs scraping.

The happiest sound in the world
Must be a baby chuckling.

Georgina Mobbs (11)
Kingswode Hoe School

The World Of Sounds

The tiniest sound in the world
Must be the book pages flapping in the breeze.

The spookiest sound in the world
Must be a tiger roaring at me.

The noisiest sound in the world
Must be a balloon banging next to me.

The happiest sound in the world
Must be an alarm clock ringing for my birthday.

Jordan Shults (12)
Kingswode Hoe School

The Sounds In The World

The tiniest sound in the world
Must be a bee fluttering past.

The spookiest sound in the world
Must be my mum shouting.

The noisiest sound in the world
Must be cats laughing with me.

The happiest sound in the world
Must be children going to play games.

Bruno Simoes Da Cruz (11)
Kingswode Hoe School

World Sounds

The tiniest sound in the world
Must be a fly tiptoeing on my knee.

The spookiest sound in the world
Must be a zombie melting in front of me.

The noisiest sound in the world
Must be a man screaming at me.

The happiest sound in the world
Must be when I tickle my nephew and he laughs cheekily.

Gareth Brady (11)
Kingswode Hoe School

Music

Music makes me tap my feet
I think that it's pretty neat.
Music makes you change your hair
Music makes you choose what to wear
Music makes you wanna fight
Music makes you feel alright.

Joseph McGee (12)
Maltings Academy

This Is Radio Clash

When I wake up in the morning,
I listen to the beaty, catchy music.
This is a punk slash rock style music
This is the Clash!

Drums fill the radio air,
Like a concert in my home.
The radio jumps in time,
As Joe Strummer hits the strings.

The beat gets quicker,
Like a car in a race.
Music gets louder,
Magnificent 7 ends sadly with a bang.

Joe shouts, 'Thank you and good night,'
Like it's the end of the Clash.
Then the beaty drum beat comes,
Like a really common cold.

'Now it's time for London Calling!'
Oh yes, my favourite song.
It rips through the speakers,
Floorboards start banging.

'Woooh,' I shout,
Enjoying my favourite song in the world.
What? The electric has just gone off,
I knew I should have paid that bill.

Adam Piper (12)
Maltings Academy

Music

M usic is so great everyone loves it
U 2 is my favourite band also many more
S ometimes I don't listen to it but I mostly do
I like it so does everyone else in my family
C alling my friends over to listen to my busting tunes.

George Hull (12)
Maltings Academy

Music

That lovely, gentle sound,
Beating all through the ground,
The incredible beat,
Makes me want to stand,
With this sound you're always on your feet.

Music, music brings me joy,
Music, music as fun as a toy,
Music, music puts me in a trance,
Music, music makes me dance.

Music is beauty to your ears,
As the crowd cheers,
From music in the club,
To music in the pub,
We all love music.

Tommy King (12)
Maltings Academy

Music

Music can be good
Music can be rubbish
Music can be loud
Music can be quiet.

There is such a variety
But I think drums are the best of them all
I just think that they are cool,
I like to listen to music when I am playing pool.

From bass to snare
Hi hat to tom tom
I love hitting them all
In one cool heat
To make up a rhythm.

Thomas Johnson (12)
Maltings Academy

Buddy Holly

Music is my favourite
Music is the best
Music makes me want to
Dance like a fool.

Music is fun
Music is cool
My favourite is rock
Pop and hip sucks socks
50s, 60s, 70s, 80s, 90s.

Modern, funk and some punk
My favourite is an instrument you strum
You've guessed it there's only one
The guitar, my faithful one.

Mark Mead (12)
Maltings Academy

Music

I love music,
All the different sounds,
I prefer football,
Because I have a kick around.

And singing and dancing to the sound,
Kicking and running all over the pitch,
All the different notes to play,
From the room I hear a high pitch.

Music is good because of all the singers
Alto, trebor, soprano, lass,
Music is good because people dance,
Music appeals in every race.

Sam English (12)
Maltings Academy

School

School, I love school
I think it's so cool
What's the point in messing about
And getting sent out
I don't get that
Why behave like a brat
I love learning
Because it'll get you earning
I copy what adults are doing
I like to copy how they're moving
I like doing sport
Every sort
I want to get a good mark in a test
Get better than the rest
I want to make hip-hop
Be on the top
I want to find a girl that wants to be with a singer
And later put a ring round her finger
I'll get all that if I go to school
Then later I'll own a swimming pool
Not be sleeping on a stool
I'll be able to act cool.

Lorenzo Korta-Haupt & Benjamin Smith (12)
Ormiston Park Academy

Untitled

Yeah it's Ray from the station
My plan is to rule the nation
I am a little impatient
I need to get an invitation
To go and rule the nation.
Yeah, that's Ray from the station
Yeah I'm from the East End
Rolling with Tyrone and Prem
Yeah and we're messing with the West End.
Yeah, that's gonna finish in a bloodbath.

Jaye Willams (12)
Ormiston Park Academy

My Friends

My friends are great,
They are so cool,
They make me giggle,
But not always do they rule!

They call me in class,
They get me told off,
They send me rude messages,
They say to me, 'I wish you would get lost.'

All day I put up with it,
It gets on my nerves.
Just because I do good in class,
They say, 'You're such a nerd!'

In science they play around with the gas,
In maths they call out my name.
In English they make up stupid sayings,
The teachers say, 'They're such a pain.'

But I still hang around with them,
Although they giggle at the sight of me,
They are still my friends,
Even though they bully.

Tiffany Ruane (12) & Samantha Joe Martin (13)
Ormiston Park Academy

Rap, It's Rap

Rap, rap, it's all about rap
If you want to come and listen just sit on my lap.
If you don't know where we are just grab a map.

It's got a beat just sing along,
Trust me I won't get it wrong.
It's got a beat, just sing along,
It may be long,
Just come along.

Rap, rap, it's all about rap.

Nicola Lewis (13)
Ormiston Park Academy

Untitled

Holidays, holidays
They're great you know
Holidays, holidays
You get to stay up late and play all day.

Holidays, holidays
You get to spend time with your family,
Holidays, holidays
Sit back and relax.

Holidays, holidays
Go fly on a plane
Holidays, holidays
Go to Spain.

Holidays, holidays
Go in the pool
Holidays, holidays
The last day today.

School, school
I've got it on Monday
School, school
I've got a while till next holiday

Lauren Ward (12)
Ormiston Park Academy

Just Be Who You Want To Be

If you be who you want to be
You wouldn't have to hide
Take a bit of pride
You're a good friend
When it comes to ends
Don't worry about trends
Don't worry about a friend
Worry about yourself
Don't ever forget be who you want to be.

Natasha Louise Smith (12)
Ormiston Park Academy

My Life Was A Mistake

I live in a dump
No self respect
Why can't I be perfect?
I live in a box
It's not even fit for a fox
Not a lot to live for . . .

Although I have a lot of friends
My life is a dump
I want some money
Can't you see?

Mummy and Daddy gone walkies
And while they are out my brother tell porkies
He says they'll be back
I know it's not true.
What else can I do?
Bye for now,
See you somehow.

Scarlet Anderson (12)
Ormiston Park Academy

When I Get Home From School

When I get home from school, I go and hide in my room
Then I hear her coming, coming towards me
I wonder what she is going to do this time.

Suddenly I whimper and try to hide
But there's nowhere to hide
Then I see her with her hard leather sole.

'I got a letter from school today,'
And she raises the shoe and it goes down with a *thump!*
And again and again until I'm black and blue all over.

I lie there crying
Thinking that tomorrow
It will happen again tomorrow but harder.

Beth Fisk (12)
Ormiston Park Academy

Me, Myself And I?

I used to be alone, but now I am at school,
I am considered quite cool.
I like to shop,
Because I have the latest trends.
I also like to hang out with my friends!
The music I listen to is not crap,
Rock and roll, hip-hop beats, but don't forget the banging rap.

School, yeah school, it may seem uncool
I think it's great, what's with all the hate?
Learning is quite cool to me, so when I'm older
I can be what I want to be!

My family is caring, my family is kind,
So I feel I can speak my mind.
When I am with them I feel fine,
And I know that they will always be mine.

Kara Cross & Molly Russell (12)
Ormiston Park Academy

Mum

Just because I don't see you anymore Mum,
It doesn't mean I forgot you,
Now that you have been gone for two years,
It doesn't mean you have to be sad.

I am fine Mum,
So is Dad,
So don't worry about it,
'Cause it is all right.

I am strong,
So are your family,
That 'cause you died two years ago,
It doesn't mean I have forgotten you.

Caitlin Harmony Rice (12)
Ormiston Park Academy

That's Life!

Some people walk the streets, singing to music and slamming beats,
While others sit around at night, healing their pain from the gansta fight.
I sit around in the empty streets, I hear the bang and running feet,
I wonder what's going on, until I hear the death song,
I know they do it for fun, but I wish that the one that dies is the one with the gun.

Some people live happy lives, while others sit around with wounds from knives,
They can go home but they're scared to walk at night alone,
So they sit there with fear in the night waiting in the street with fright.

The world is full of horror and crime, but we have to live with it
I guess it's called life.

Simone Georgia Hibbert (12)
Ormiston Park Academy

Life As A Teen

Life as a teen is rough,
It seems that it's all about sex, drugs and violence.
What do you think?
People getting boyfriends and girlfriends trying to be cool,
But all that happens is that you get kicked out of school.

Life at home is just as bad cos all you hear are your parents arguing
And never getting along.

I know it's hard and
I know it's tough but
If you start with yourself
I know you'll make a change
Think about it.

Sharon Sangotade (12)
Ormiston Park Academy

Just Because

Just because I am weird, it doesn't mean I am not normal.
Just because I get good grades, it doesn't mean I am a nerd.
Just because I haven't smoked or taken drugs,
It doesn't mean I am not cool.
Just because I had not picked real friends,
It doesn't mean I am a loser.
Just because I don't fight,
It doesn't mean I am a loser.

I am who I am, and this is who I'll forever be.
I do not care what others think of me.
Like me or not it is your choice
Accept me for who I am.

Luke Capstick (12)
Ormiston Park Academy

Why Me?

Why me, why us?
A world with guns and drugs.
Who is the cause?
What is the cause?
Young boys talking the hardest,
But do they know that actions speak louder than words?
Mothers, fathers wondering where the hell their child is,
But really they're on the way rushing to the hospital.
But really what I'm saying is
You can do it, go for it and make a change.
No one can stop you now!

Aaron Agyekum (12)
Ormiston Park Academy

Just Because!

Just because I'm annoying doesn't mean I am not a good friend.
Just because I have got lots of enemies,
Doesn't mean I haven't got friends.
Just because I am friends with the people you hate,
Doesn't mean you have to hate me.
Just because I used to be horrible doesn't mean I haven't changed.
Just because I don't smoke, doesn't mean I am not cool.
Just because I hang about with boys doesn't mean I go out with them.
And I'm never going to change for you,
So if you don't accept me for who I am
Don't accept me at all.

Chloe Ferguson (12)
Ormiston Park Academy

Drugs

We use them and we abuse them
We get high
So don't use them.
Gangsters use them, adults use them
But they always blame the gangster
But not the youth but never the adults.

Fern Skingley (12)
Ormiston Park Academy

Abused

A ttacked, beaten, slapped, it's all happened to me
B roken-hearted, I won't let anyone touch me
U nder the kitchen table hiding, my heart's pounding,
    praying to God she won't hurt me
S he apologises but I know she will do it again
E ach day goes by not knowing what to do next, not knowing who to tell
D epressed and hurt, I feel like my life is over.

Jadesola Olopade (14)
Park School for Girls

My Nan

Well my nan,
She's not like others,
A cigarette for breakfast,
And a tea full of sugar.

She starts her day,
With shouts and scream,
Talks funny English,
She doesn't know what she means.

Her favourite pastime
Is to cook,
We have to eat it,
No matter how it looks.

So many relatives,
Don't get me started,
Excuses for gatherings,
Can't wait till they've departed.

She smokes so much,
That she stinks,
It affects her health,
But she doesn't think.

Although I say all these things,
I really do love her,
After all she is my gran,
I would prefer no other.

Sehyr Sarfaraz (12)
Park School for Girls

My Mum Keeps On Telling Me

My mum keeps on telling me,
She works hard all day and it drags!
She always says she's as busy as a bee,
But the only thing she does is brag!

She tells me to grow up!
When I want to be silly,
Then I would look up,
And say,
'Please Lord always keep her busy!'

My mum always says,
'Keep up with your studies!'
As every day I bring home,
Lots of my buddies!

She scares them off,
By showing them pens and books.
They run away,
By my mum's scary looks!

My mum keeps on telling me,
'What I say is always true,
I always want you to listen to me,
Because I love you!'

Dilshad Adam (12)
Park School for Girls

Violence

From my sight,
I see people fight.
From what I hear,
People swear.
From what I smell,
I can tell.
That when people drink,
They never think.
From what I feel,
It's really real.
You see those knives,
They're taking people's lives.
There's violence out there,
But people don't care.
Some do,
It gives them the shivers too.
I can't get out there, not alone,
I have to stay safe in my home.

Aaliya Farook Oomerjee (12)
Park School for Girls

Fears

When spiders are crawling up the door
When the rats are running across the floor
All the fears of them come to me like nothing imagined at all,
When the lights are switched off at night,
When the owls are howling with fright
I sit in my bed while nightmares about me fall.
When the doors creak,
When the floorboards squeak.
It makes me feel someone's around,
I run to my mum and sit by her side.
The sweat is running down my face
As if I am in a running race.
Crouching up and getting scared
As if my boat's sinking in a tide.

Soha Nadeem (11)
Park School for Girls

Owls

Hoot! Hoot! cry the birds of prey
I hate their claws, they are rather sharp I say
I can see their dark, scary shadows on my bedroom wall
I can hear their loud, eerie call
The flyers of the night
The birds of fright
Their dreadful howl
Their smell so foul
Their claws designed to rip and tear
And strip their unfortunate prey bare
I lay in bed
Turning my head
At every sound they make
Why am I so frightened? For Heaven's sake
I can't sleep peacefully and ignore them for once
They ignore us even when we are in abundance
I'm really annoyed because these owls you see
Are definitely haunting me!

Harini Anand (13)
Park School for Girls

Abused

She is there but who will care?
Kids like her are not that rare.
She is being bullied at school,
Because she's not cool.
Someone come and give her a hand,
Can't you see she is being buried in the sand?
She is trying to scream and shout,
But there is no one about.
She is being abused,
There's proof she has been bruised.
When will they stop?
If they don't she will go mad and drop,
Then they will see what harm they have done.
Now all she can do is *run!*

Maria Farook Oomerjee (13)
Park School for Girls

Malta

As I stand on the cliff top,
And gaze out across the land,
The blue sea sparkles,
And sunrays come tumbling down.

Soft and silky is the sand,
That lies around this stunning land,
Dolphins swim and jump and wave,
Not far from where the children play.

Ever heard of the Blue Lagoon?
Well this is where it is,
Down you dive and the sea comes alive,
Teeming with fish and coral.

The heat here is intense,
As the sun is always shining,
My favourite place in the world,
Malta!

Sophie Caruana (13)
Park School for Girls

War

Bombs, bombs fall from the sky like gigantic drops of rain,
Filling the streets with hurt and devastating pain.
Piles of rubble everywhere, no place left safe.
Bodies, bodies lying dead in the crowded street,
From children to men bleeding in the searing heat.
'Mummy, Mummy, please wake up, stop bleeding now, don't leave me.'
To the land where angels and dead people can forever be free.
Crying, crying everywhere, not one face left dry,
Loved ones dead and their families howling to the dark filled skies.
'My child she's gone, oh dear, oh my! How will I live on?'
'You may not live on my precious dear until the war has gone.'
War, war, I've seen it all I've survived the worst,
I'd give my life to those children who really need it first.
It's not right to toy with people's lives,
The world's red, it's filled with blood spread across the skies.

Sabrina Fearon Melville (11)
Park School for Girls

The Autumn

Whirling leaves yellow and brown
On the ground and in the town
Leaves are everywhere up and down
The king even has leaves in his crown.

The leaves are colourful and fluffy
And it never ever feels stuffy
They crunch and crunch under my feet
To walk outside is a real treat.

It is a cold and rainy day
The children pray they can play
They give up and say okay
The children try to stay away.

The leaves become soft and sticky
They stick to your shoes and become icky
You end up leaving muddy muddy tracks
Then you clean and clean on your breaking back.

Warner Dixon (12)
Park School for Girls

Mood Swings

Alive? Dead?
Happy? Sad?
This is how I feel,
One minute I'm alive,
And next I'm dead,
Then one minute I'm happy,
And then I'm sad
What do I do?
Black? White?
Darkness? Brightness?
This is how I feel,
One minute I'm in the dark,
And then I'm in the light.
What do I do?
I'm so confused . . .

Rohini Soni (14)
Park School for Girls

War And Peace

I woke up one day with a thought
About something I had been previously taught.
I was thinking about peace and war
And why some people are rich and some are poor.

It seemed easy to understand before
But it is a subject I don't get any more.
I used to think that's the way it works
But now I think why do people get hurt?

I live in a world with not much love
Maybe we should give peace a little shove.
But I still don't understand all the fighting
And I am tired of all the political writing.

Now why can't everyone just get along?
The leaders are all selfish and wrong.
As the years stroll by in preparation
Leading the world to peace, the next generation.

Saffiyah Omar (12)
Park School for Girls

School Is Boring!

S chool is boring, all we do is work
C an there be an even worse place huh? No way
H omework every day, non stop
O bliged to do it every day
O h my gosh I'm going to explode
L ate at school, I get told off!

I hate school!
S ometimes I want to pull my hair out!

B ut no one lets me
O h what horrid food, I'd
R ather eat worms
I hate school
N othing but torture
G oodness! What am I going to do?

Saleha Ahmed (12)
Park School for Girls

Hallowe'en

On 31st October the things you must do,
Is pretend that nothing can scare you.
If you can't handle it and you want to run,
Just remember it's Hallowe'en fun.

'Hallowe'en's fun!' I hear you say,
Let me explain, if I may,
The witches go riding and black cats are seen,
All because of Hallowe'en.

Ghosts and goblins, skeletons and bats,
Don't be afraid of all of that.
This is all make-believe,
Funny costumes on Hallowe'en.

The children knock from door to door,
'Trick or treat?' Treats galore!
Homeward bound, a job well done,
Can't wait 'til next time, fun, fun, fun!

Prabhjot Kaur (12)
Park School for Girls

Evil Bogeys

E ven though I say 'Be nice'
V enom runs through her veins
I promise myself I'll get her back though
L ethal ones think first.

B ad, bad, bad is what goes on in her head
O h, why did I ask for her?
'G ood girl' is what they call her, but
E ven I know deep down inside
Y ucky green things
S lither around in her head.

T his is how I describe my little sister
A nd many others do too
B ut just remember they're trying to say
'I really do love you!'

Shayla Reid (12)
Park School for Girls

Hallowe'en

Going out in the frosty air
I wonder what would happen there?
Ghosts and ghouls is what I expect
I wonder what will happen next.

Little children everywhere
Screaming, here and there
Everyone's excited, adults too
All dressed up as happy as the children too.

I love Hallowe'en, it's the best
You'll never know what will happen next,
Wizards and witches will follow you,
Even when you're in the loo.

Don't be scared or afraid
It only lasts a day
Enjoy it while it's there
Because it's here, there and everywhere.

Ammarah Wali (12)
Park School for Girls

Dance

Dancing is the best
Dancing beats the rest
Dancing is a passion
Dancing is active
Dancing is bouncy and jumpy
Dancing is creative
Dancing is adventurous
In a group or alone
In a room or in a hall
Wherever you are
Whoever you're with
Happy or sad
Hot or cold
Dancing never gets old.

Monisha Mehta (12)
Park School for Girls

I'm Not Happy

I'm not happy because I've lost my socks
I'm not happy because I caught the chickenpox
I'm not happy because an insect flew by
I'm not happy my skirt flew up high
I'm not happy because apparently I smell bad
I'm not happy because my mum thinks I'm mad
I'm not happy because my hair is a mess
I'm not happy I look guilty as you can guess
I'm not happy there's a spider on my bed
I'm not happy an egg landed on my head
I'm not emo, so don't think that
I just get bullied because I'm so fat
I feel like the need to cry
Why am I thinking this? I don't know why
I'll just add a smile to my day
It'll keep me happy all the way.

Caroline Cheung (13)
Park School for Girls

All Alone

It's winter time now and I am seven.
I pull my boots on and head for the door.
Do my parents miss me up in Heaven?
I go outside and head for the moor.
I'm surrounded by snow,
And I really miss my dad.
There's a pain in each toe
Like the pain in my heart. It hurts so bad.
I long to be home where it's safe,
Back with my mum and dad.
I trudge my way back, a lonely waif,
But they're with God. Why should I feel sad?
I arrive back at home.
A tear trickles down my cheek.
As I sit on my own,
Daddy's little lamb so timid and meek.

Karishma Desai (11)
Park School for Girls

Mind, Body And Soul

My mind is as cloudy as dry ice,
My body is as functional as a robot,
But my soul's as serene as pasture's symphony.
My mind won't ever stop demanding,
My body won't ever stop working,
But the soul, my friend, won't ever stop loving.
My mind can't be focussed and calm,
My body keeps me healthy and alive,
But really, my soul keeps me going.
My mind's an untamed, hyper devil,
My body's a real smart angel,
But my soul's my forever Paradise City.
My mind is a realy busy swimming pool,
My body is a teardrop manufacturer,
But my soul's as placid as Arctic ice.
My mind, body and soul makes me - Simmy D!

Simran Dev (12)
Park School for Girls

Confused

The sun is shining,
The birds are singing,
What about me?
My ears are ringing!
Argue, argue, argue,
All day long,
Next thing you know, they're gone!
My head feels like it's burning,
My mind is rapidly turning.
I'm, lying on my bed,
What have I got to dread?
I'm terribly tired,
My mum just got fired!
Well it isn't all that bad,
So why am I so sad?
I guess I could make this feeling fly away.

Sara Siabi (13)
Park School for Girls

Why?

Why does this always happen to me?
Can't she just leave me alone?
I want to be like everyone else.

Pressure builds up and up,
As she shouts out to me,
Every time I feel like speaking out,
My feelings put me down.

I want to learn, but not too much,
Or I'll be called a 'teacher's pet',
Are they jealous? Or is it just their game?

I know I'm not stylish,
I know I don't fit in,
I'm not like them,
But that's just me! Why should I change?

Shashiwadana Kariyakarawana (14)
Park School for Girls

Feelings

We all have feelings both me and you
Sometimes we feel happy
Sometimes we feel sad
Sometimes we love
Sometimes we hate
Sometimes we're excited
Sometimes we're proud of something we have achieved.
Sometimes we're angry
Sometimes miserable
Sometimes we feel pity
Sometimes we feel sorry
Sometimes we're anxious
Sometimes we're curious
These are feelings both you and me feel.

Mahham Mukhtar (13)
Park School for Girls

They . . .

They make him cry,
They think he's dry,
They trip him up,
They knocked him flat,
They made him sad, like an old door mat,
They kick him around,
They knock him to the ground,
They make him frown,
They think they're a clown,
They all take a turn,
They all make him burn,
They follow him to the shop,
But will they eventually stop?

Zara Kaur (13)
Park School for Girls

Untitled

Snow White is happy,
But Sleeping Beauty is sad.
Shrek is angry
And Fiona is mad.

We all have feelings,
The famous too
Happy and sad
Like me and you.

Some are cheeky
And some are sly.
Some are happy
And some cry.

Rumaanah Sajid Tailor (13)
Park School for Girls

I Love Animals . . .

I n little baskets, kennels or even in the house

L ots of different types
O ver the world, making people like me happy
V ery special and unique
E very animal has the magic touch

A nimals are there to love and hug
N ot to hurt or abandon
I n different colours, different sizes
M edium, large or small
A ny size is perfect for me, they are all
L oving, cute, caring and
S oft, soft, soft.

Mica Mehta (12)
Park School for Girls

My Brother

Scratches, pinches, bellows and shouts
Running, jumping, screaming about
Eating chocolates and eating sweets
Exercise is out and games are in
Killings, murders, games of all kinds
Upset every time he gives you a kick
Take his PSP and he will feel sick
Talkative and lazy, always a fool
All he is good for is to be put in the bin
Nutty and rude, all he is

    PS I really love him.

Vrindha Venn (13)
Park School for Girls

Polar Bears

P oor polar bears get killed for skin!
O h my gosh how bad of us
L arge white bears
A re slowly getting *extinct!*
R emember! Polar.

B ears are living creatures too!
E ven though they are meat eaters they
A lso have a right to live
R are 'n' mighty but
S oft 'n' furry too!
    So why not help me save 'em?

Shreyashi Verma (12)
Park School for Girls

Families

F amilies are your friend, not just your brother, sister or parents
A lways behind you, in the sun or in the rain, they'll be there for you
M ums are wonderful. When you were young, who cared for you? your mum
I nside you, you love your siblings but you don't want to show it
L ove. Everyone hates their brother or sister, but at the end of the day you care for them
I call my brother names but I still love him
E njoy. Family is about enjoying each other because when they're gone they won't come back
S afe and sound. The safest place to be is your home with your family.

Sana Patel (12)
Park School for Girls

Me!

I am me,
That's who I am,
Walking round the city,
Eating cooked ham!
I like to dance,
It's just what I do,
Moving my feet,
How about you?
I have a brother and sister,
They're quite small,
Obviously that's not me,
I'm very tall!
I get quite hungry,
Eat lots of food,
Well it really depends
Whether I'm in the right mood!
I love my family,
We have a great laugh,
I even find it funny when I'm in the bath!
I love to swim,
Just up and down the pool,
Sliding and gliding,
I think I'm cool!
I am me,
That's who I am,
Walking round the city,
Eating cooked ham!

Emily Henderson (12)
Redden Court School

I'm Not Sober

Slowly fading,
Brain imploding,
Going crazy,
Vision fading,
Stop.
Slowly trudging through the rain,
To try real hard but for no gain.
Go to clinics far and wide,
But I'm still numb inside.
As soon as the alcohol touches your lips,
For your life, that is it.
Try to remember to forget
Whiskey shots and cheap cigarettes.
Rushed to hospital, body in pain,
I guess all the alcohol put me in strain.
Face-masked women, treating the men,
But I'll never the same again.

Slowly fading,
Brain imploding,
Going crazy,
Vision fading,
Stop.

Harry Rogers (12)
Redden Court School

Friendship

What is a friend?
A friend is like a spirit that never goes away.
A friend is like a gate that never comes unlatched.
A friend is like a link that you can't rub out.
A friend has been there from the start,
And hopefully to the end.
A friend will pull you aside if something isn't right.

A friend will do all of this
And will be like this if they are a friend.

Georgina Martin (13)
Redden Court School

Don't!

Don't be worried,
Don't be sad,
Don't be angry,
Don't be mad.

Don't hold grudges,
And don't be rude,
And remember the world goes on.

Be happy,
And jolly,
And laugh all the time,
Enjoy your life,
And make friends along the line.

So . . .
Don't be worried,
Don't be sad,
Don't be angry,
Don't be mad.

Don't hold grudges,
And don't be rude,
And remember the world goes on.

Chelsea Huggins (13)
Redden Court School

A True Friend

A true friend will listen if you have something to say.
A true friend will be there for you every single day
A true friend will remember you long after you die.

A true friend will be there for you when you need them the most.
A true friend is like a teddy, you hug them when you're upset.

A true friend won't boast when they buy a gift.
A true friend will remember you long after you die.

Friends from the start, friends 'til the end
I hope you like this poem about a true friend.

Gemma Brooks (13)
Redden Court School

Where Have You Gone?

Where have you gone?
I want to know
Are you OK?
Please tell me so.

Where are you now?
In a good place or bad?
How are you feeling?
Angry or sad?

Did you give up?
Or did it take hold?
Were you too tired
To keep going on?

I just want to know
I need some peace
I've had so much hurt
I just want to live.

Do not worry
I won't forget
The times that we shared
The memories you've left.

Sarah Eost (12)
Redden Court School

Hallowe'en

Scary ghost next to the post
I'm really scared as it has horrible hair
It gives me a right scare.

Hallowe'en, Hallowe'en.

It's that time of year again
And it makes me so frightened
I have to write a rhyme
And have some playtime.

Hallowe'en, Hallowe'en.

Chloe Wade (13)
Redden Court School

My Hero, My Dad!

For years I've had a hero
That I didn't really know
But I remember him so well
As if I saw him two days ago.

He was a dad to me
And a good one too
He did everything for us
And with a smile too.

He fought for years
With an illness so strong
But he never gave up
And still stayed strong.

When it finally beat him
I was so upset
My dad was gone
But he's still my hero yet.

I will never forget him
He meant so much to me
He'll always be my hero
And someone special to me.

Megan Brown (12)
Redden Court School

Dave Grohl

D rummer
A nd
V ocalist
E xcellent

G uitar
R ocker
O utstanding
H onour
L ong road to ruin.

Sean Nicolaides (11)
Redden Court School

Friends Forever!

Some friends are close,
Some friends are like sisters,
Some friends are pen pals,
Some friends are distant,
Friends forever!

Some friends are annoying,
Some friends are funny,
Some friends are smart,
Some friends are crazy,
Friends forever!

Some friends are tall,
Some friends are cruel,
Some friends are small,
Some friends just rule,
Friends forever!

All friends are different,
And I like it that way,
Friends forever,
That's all I can say!

Emily Hart (12)
Redden Court School

Friendship

Friendship is great when you have friends
Friendship is unhappy when you have sad moments
I think friendship is a great experience to have.
Also true friends will listen to each other.
True friends will be there for you every single day or hour.
Friends will always look up to you when you are feeling down,
So always be there to give a hand.
You should always have a true friend,
So when you are down they will always have a chat so make it last.
When your friend is by your side, let them always share your pride.
You and your friend share jokes and laughter,
That means you will live happily ever after.

Karis Davey (13)
Redden Court School

I Wish

I fill up with anger when I see them,
When they come near I wish I could push them away.
They stare at me, I stare back,
This argument is going on forever, I wish it would stop.

Sitting in class seems like forever,
Sitting as far away as I can.
It is so silent you could hear a pin drop,
This argument is going on forever, I wish it would stop.

I cry a river,
I throw books against my wall.
Bang! Crash!
This argument is going on forever, I wish it would stop.

We spoke today,
It's all over.
No more grudges, no more sadness,
This argument was going on forever.
No more tears, no more heartache,
We belong together.

Heather Eldridge (12)
Redden Court School

Cheryl Cole

As she walks out of the hotel the paparazzi come swarming
Getting the shot to make a story.
Having people turn their back on her,
Still sharing that glowing smile,
Whilst having her dream come true.
She grew.
Cheryl Cole . . .
Sparkling eyes
Lushy, shiny hair.
The angel of the north,
The nations' sweetheart,
Solo artist,
My heroine.

Danielle Aubrey-Tootell (12)
Redden Court School

Families

Christmas Day, hooray, hooray
A million times we say
Hooray, hooray.
Waking up and opening presents
Eating dinner with family and pulling crackers
What wonderful time with family.

Wake up one day and it's your birthday
Opening presents and blowing out candles
Having fun with friends and family
What wonderful time with family.

It's a holiday, oh boy, oh boy!
On the beach and riding roller coasters, going swimming
And going out for dinner
What wonderful time with family.

The family have won
And have had lots of fun
What wonderful time with family.

Joseph Brewer (12)
Redden Court School

He's My Hero

Bang . . .
In a war zone
Dead on the ground.
He was funny,
Humorous.
Uncle, Uncle,
Why was it you?
You're the best
My hero.
The hero.
He risked it,
His life for his country
Most importantly . . .
For me!

Ria Smyth (11)
Redden Court School

Life

I am surrounded by
Arguing, fighting, crime,
Anger, pain and hurt.
Why? I ask one question: why?

Life is a gift,
Use it wisely.
Don't be sad, be happy.
Why? I ask one question: why?

Sadness is what I live in,
Yes, sadness.
I hope in time I will brighten up.
Why? I ask one question.

I will brighten up, I will, I will.
But for now I have to live.
Hurt, crime, anger and pain, why?
I ask one question: why?
Why?

Louise Garraway (12)
Redden Court School

My Hero

Excellent
Best player
Brilliant
Skills and tricks leave players standing
Good control
Likes Spanish league
Fools players
42 goals, not a problem
Worth 80 millions pounds
Free kick master
Four clubs Sporting Lisbon, Real Madrid, Man U, Portugal
Right wing is his position
Playmaker for all his teams
Immense.

Sean Callum Jacks (11)
Redden Court School

My Cat

Tail flicking
Milk licking,
Very cuddly,
Soft and snuggly.

Black and white,
Out all night.
Ginger Tom,
Where's he gone?

Shiny eyes,
Big surprise,
Long whiskers,
Purring whispers.

Chasing birds,
How absurd!
Fluffy and fat,
That's my cat!

Jessica Russell (12)
Redden Court School

My Grandma

Grandma,
She is kind,
Helpful,
She's always funny,
Happy,
She never gives up,
But when you're sad she'll make you happy,
I love my grandma and she loves me,
She understands me when I'm sad,
My grandma has tons of beans and so do I,
She always sings to me,
She loves cooking, so do I,
I love you Grandma because you're great
I love you
You're the love fairy!

Chloe Palmer-Anscomb (11)
Redden Court School

A Sailor's Life

Waving slowly across the rough seas,
Sailors working on their knees,
Yellow coats and yellow hats,
Make the sailors look so fat!

The waves then stop,
And everything calms,
Walk out on the deck
And nothing is harmed.

You are so pleased to live another day,
Go home to your wife with your pay,
Stepping off the boat, you're home,
Walk in the door, you are not alone.

Back out to sea you go,
Watching the blue, just flow,
Catching fish, tasty cod,
That's the way to cast a rod.

Louie Hak (12)
Redden Court School

Cristiano Ronaldo

Shoot!
Cristiano Ronaldo,
Smash to goal,
Free kick superstar,
80 million move to Madrid.

He played for four clubs,
Lisbon, Man U, Madrid, Portugal,
Broke the net,
Cristiano Ronaldo
Skilful.

Ronaldo,
Skilful shooter,
Fast as lightning,
Ronaldo! Ronaldo! Ronaldo! Ronaldo!

Ben Hunt (11)
Redden Court School

God Knows The Reason Why!

They call me names
I hide my head in shame
They say I'm sad and lame
But all they want is, attention or fame.

They hit and punch
Then I cry
God knows the reason why!
What did I do
That was so wrong?
But I've got to carry on.

They think they're tough
But I've had enough
I know I'm not to blame
They should hang their heads in shame!

I should feel sorry for these guys
God knows the reason why!

Sophy Bakal (13)
Redden Court School

I Like Football

I like to play football
All players, short and tall
Doesn't matter if you're rich or poor
You should always know the score

Running like a cheetah down the pitch
Running for the ball like an old disgruntled witch
It brings the family together
In all sorts of weather.

I like to play football
All players, short and tall
15 minutes, halftime
All fits in their rhyme.

But some people like rugby.

Jack Collins (14)
Redden Court School

My Wii

I love playing the Nintendo Wii,
It makes me feel so happy,
All of the games are really fun,
My favourite one is Mario Kart Wii!

I like playing on it with friends,
It makes it even more fun!
I don't want to ever stop playing it,
I like it so much!

There are so many different games to play,
My friends always want to stay,
So they can play on it all day!

Everybody likes playing on the Wii,
Including me!
No one can really dislike the Wii,
Not when you can make your very own Mii!

Shannon Barrett (12)
Redden Court School

Ned

I am a teddy bear, my name is Ned,
Dusty and lonely, I'm under the bed
The family dog is called Benjamin
I smell all the food from his dog food tin
One day he came in and sat on my head
I hardly could breathe, he covered my head
I cried a tear and it tasted of salt
Nobody loves me, well that's what I thought
The days and nights crept by like a snail
I was left in the dark with Mr Whale
One eye on my face, one ear on my head
How much I wanted to be on Billy's bed
One day when it was cold, the sharp wind blew
I was on the bed again, then I knew
I was loved like before, and on the bed
I am a teddy bear, my name is Ned!

Georgina Newland (12)
Redden Court School

New York City

New York is the place to be,
Lots of lights and sights to see,
Cars and buses
Fill the street,
The sound of workers on their feet.
A hot dog stand smell fills the air,
Tourists stare at Lady Liberty who now lives there,
You see the homeless in the shelters,
Thank the charities who pay for the helpers.
The parks are green and nice as can be,
The families picnic under the oak tree,
Take a ride through the middle at night,
You won't notice the stars because it's so light.

Lots of lights and sights to see,
That's why New York is the place to be.

Adam Hewitt (13)
Redden Court School

Football Players

F ootball crazy, football mad
O n the pitch they wish
O ne in goal, ten out field
T hierry Henry, he doesn't like fish
B ecause they appeal they get booked
A ppeal again they get sent off
L ove the game
L ive the game.

P layers moan and groan
L oved by all
A shley Young
Y ou will win and lose
E verybody today
R ed and yellow are the cards
S how racism the red card!

Lewis Jaggs (11)
Redden Court School

My Dad

My dad's my hero,
He never gives zero.
He's my dad,
But he's not a bad dad.
My dad's the best,
He gives me tests.
He works hard,
He plays in the yard.
My dad eats the best,
He hates all the rest.
He always takes dares,
But he cares.
He loves mats,
But hates cats.

Lee Andre Aglae (11)
Redden Court School

West Ham United

W est Ham are the best
E very time beating the rest
S ometimes losing we sing, *'Boohoo!'*
T ime is following us, following you.

H is name is Sir Bobby Moore
A nd he won the FA after the war
M anchester United, they usually win

U sually they try to kick the ball in
N ever give up
I want us to win the Cup
T ops and shorts usually get muddy
E ventually at least one player gets a new buddy
D anger of score at full time.

Ronnie Charles David Higgs (11)
Redden Court School

My Dream

My dream,
My dream is to own a really big house in a faraway land,
Where it is as quiet as a mouse,
Where ponies will graze on the hill,
Right outside the old mill.

Birds will cheep in the trees
As I ride my chestnut horse in the autumn leaves,
As the golden brown leaves start to drop,
The horses' hooves go *clip, clop*.

The wind chimes jingle
In the calm autumn breeze,
Where I sit by the window,
Just wondering, *will I ever get that dream?*

Holly Venton (12)
Redden Court School

My Brother

I have a brother,
Whose name is Adam,
He is fifteen years old,
We have always argued
Since I was one year old!

Me and my brother argue because
We wind each other up,
It always ends with him winning,
So he thinks he's won the cup.

He could always be a better brother,
If he just didn't wind me up,
And if we didn't ever fight,
We could always try to make up!

Ryan Johnson (13)
Redden Court School

My Sister

My sister, I look up to her,
She's my role model,
I look up to her when I need her.

She listens to my thoughts and feelings,
I care for her when she's in danger.

My sister is my heroine,
She's a joyful person,
We have our ups and downs,
But we always make up.

At the end of forever,
She's my sister
And I love her!

Stacey Marie Tonks (13)
Redden Court School

When The Day Is Done

Raining days are just so fun
But in the end it's
Not so fun
The bun of life
May just be done
Because during rain
The death toll gains
Because in the end
We all just die
But who cares now?
It's all just fun
Because it's raining
The day is done.

Rhys Floyde (13)
Redden Court School

My Nan

My nan is my heroine
She inspired me to cook
Everything my nan is
Something rubs off on me
I think the part of cooking
Is what's part of me
We always like the taste
I love my nan lots
She loves me lots
We are together a lot
We like to be together
We have fun whatever we do
I love you Nan.

Melissa Watts
Redden Court School

Friends

My friends are my life,
They mean everything to me,
They're trustworthy and reliable,
Together since primary.

We've had good times and fall outs
But we are still standing strong,
They're always there for me,
We'll be friends forever long.

As now I still love them
Like I will until the end of time,
They bring me joy
Like the peace of a wind chime.

Emily Lewin (12)
Redden Court School

Scary, Funny And Random Things

Scary, funny and random things,
Like spiders, balloons and flowers with wings,
A dog in a tree, bear in a house,
A seven foot cat being chased by a mouse.

Lightning and thunder on dark dreary nights,
My sister and brother in day to day fights,
Dog and cat pie, fried tiger stew,
Reading Beano whilst on the loo.

I'm happy, I'm sad, I haven't got a clue,
My mum ate my homework, I'm telling you it's true,
Scary, funny and random things,
Like spiders, balloons and flowers with wings.

Amy White (12)
Redden Court School

My Aunt

My heroine is my great aunt,
She doesn't believe in the word can't,
She is loving and caring,
She believes in sharing.

My aunt is considerate and kind,
She has done well for herself, you will find,
She donates a lot of money to charity,
She is completely clear with clarity,
Her cooking is absolutely great,
She is very patient and happy to wait.

My heroine is my great aunt,
She doesn't believe in the word can't.

Grace Caitlin Donnelly (11)
Redden Court School

Rugby

Rugby, it's a man's game,
Try and take all the pain,
Walk off at the end of the day
Then find out that you've gone over the parking fee.

Rugby, it's a long hard day,
Hearing the whistle at the end,
Maybe a cheer if you've won,
Shake their hand as a sign of respect.

Rugby, it is a dirty and muddy day,
Some broken ribs and sneaky tricks,
Long old bath, nice to relax,
A well-earned beer at the end!

Aidan Pearce (13)
Redden Court School

It's Not Us?

Why do we get the blame,
Arrested, told off, heads in shame
No one knows what it's like to be
In our shoes, living as a teen.
Nowadays we're on the news
In the spotlight, getting accused
Blame on us and being labelled
We want to work hard 'cause we are able.
It's not like you can call yourself perfect
Don't point the finger 'cause it's not worth it
So why don't you just stop and think
What it's like to be a teen?

Ellie Adams (14)
Redden Court School

My Mum

My mum is caring,
She's never nasty,
She always makes us laugh,
She's always loving,
Never upset,
She always helps us,
And never makes things difficult,
When my dad was ill,
She always cheered us up,
She's my heroine that I know
And they're the reasons why!

Midnight Millett-Bangs (11)
Redden Court School

My Hobbies

Just because I like golf doesn't mean I am old.
Just because I am good at school
Doesn't mean I'm really good and have to be told.

In PE I don't get gold,
But I can still be taught and told.
I think tennis is cool,
But after a game we always jump in the pool.

Tennis is a kid's game,
But when we are older can we put them to shame,
And it could make me have fame.

Joseph Mauceri (13)
Redden Court School

My Hero . . .

Even if I don't say a word
He knows when something is wrong
I can tell him anything
He makes me laugh so much
He helps me when I need him
There are times when I want to kill him
But I'd kill for him all the time
I wouldn't swap him for the world.

Patsi Weedon (13)
Redden Court School

Leonardo Da Vinci

D a Vinci's
A rt was

V ery
I nspirational to
N umerous
C hildren and adults
I would like to be like him.

Sam Fisk (11)
Redden Court School

My Mum

My mum is mega nice,
She's not plain like rice,
She works her socks off day and night,
She is full with might,
My mum is truly the best,
Better than the rest,
She is a hard-working nurse.

Tanya Eastwood (11)
Redden Court School

Friends

F riendship
R elationship
I s always there for us
E very day without a fuss
N ice, kind people
D oing heaps of playing
S ometimes they make you feel sad.

Lauren Jessica Froste (11)
Redden Court School

Changing Seasons

Daffodils swaying in the breeze,
Cherry blossom icing upon the trees,
The first green shoots reaching up to the sun,
Easter bunnies and hot cross buns,
Gardens fresh in the early morning dew,
Spring is all around us, crisp and new.

Fathers and children across the land,
Building castles high in the sand,
Gentle breezes softly blowing,
Gardens full of flowers growing,
Children playing in the fields,
With summer and sunshine my smile builds.

As the sun grows weaker and cools,
Smoky bonfires, witches and ghouls,
Ablaze with the colours that nature weaves,
Before the trees shake off their leaves,
Autumn takes us by the hand,
And leads us to a winter wonderland.

Wake up in the morning to a wonderful sight,
Snowflakes falling, crisp and white,
Frosty fingers tingling with cold,
Building snowmen, big and bold,
Children asleep on a winter's eve,
Dream of Santa and the presents they hope to receive.

Alice Neil (11)
St Mary's School, Colchester

Scars

Alone I sat in the cold dark room,
The evil slowly creeping through my skin
Dancing slowly through my veins
Enhancing heart, mind and soul.

As the icy dark pierced my heart
My hand slowly itched
Towards the Devil's hand
Delicately placed on my leg.

One small slice was all that was needed
To keep Satan's soul at bay
Just a few hours of peace
Enough to keep my sanity.

As I watched the scarlet creep
Working its way to say hello
I felt Satan's soul yell out
Being suppressed beneath my skin.

Washing all the blood away
I slowly looked in the mirror
Despite the few hours of peace I had
I saw the monster I'd become.

I plastered on my happy face
And stepped slowly out the door
'Me against the world,' I said
No one understands.

Alone I sat in the cold dark room
The evil slowly creeping through my skin
Dancing slowly through my veins
Enhancing heart, mind and soul.

Jess Francis (14)
St Mary's School, Colchester

Secret Hero

I enter the world of enchantment,
Clad in billowing, golden robes,
With a glinting sword at my side,
A unicorn I sit astride.

I am now in the land of mythical creatures,
Where elfin folk, sorcerers and serpents feature.
Hags, wraiths, sprites, demons, dragons in caves,
These are the dangers I have to brave.

I explore searing mountains, lakes and forests deep
I discover a wizened old warlock fast asleep
I seek ancient treasure,
I go on quests and find adventure.

I've slain an evil dragon, breathing flame,
I've cured a pegasus who was lame,
I restored a forgotten kingdom,
Many riddles have tested my wisdom.

When I return victorious creatures cheer,
No longer do they fear
Dangers or a terrible beast,
So they celebrate with a feast.

When everybody has eaten their fill,
They fall asleep and become still,
Then I steal away,
As I can no longer stay.

The next day I get up and go to school,
But don't think I'm simple, a geek or a fool,
I know I look like just a schoolgirl though,
But, in my dreams, I'm really a secret hero!

Jessica Hale (11)
St Mary's School, Colchester

Life According To Me

Life is like a footprint in the sand.
Once made,
It stays for a while,
Then slowly fades away in silence with the cradling ebb of the sea.
Life teaches us many valuable lessons,
Some good and some bad.
In life you have friends,
Who make your life a happy one.
But you have enemies too,
Who, in turn,
Make your life glum.
Can we really judge life by the things
That make it a good or bad place to be?
No one knows what life is like
Until they've lived and experienced it all.
Dying,
Just to see how life really is,
Sounds like an awful way to go.
But it happens to everyone,
It could be the greatest adventure of all.
Perhaps greater than life itself.
Life is like a footprint in the sand.
Once made,
It stays for a while,
Then slowly fades away with the cradling ebb of the sea.

Eleanor Jolliffe (13)
St Mary's School, Colchester

Separation

Sometimes I feel it's my fault,
I feel my life's unfair,
I know it's not my fault,
That my parents aren't a pair.

Sometimes I feel guilty,
I don't know wrong from right,
Mostly when I'm lonely,
I think of all those fights.

I can still remember that cold winter day,
When they sat me down and together they would say,
'I just can't cope anymore,'
Said my dad looking down,
'Me and your dad are splitting up,'
Said my mum with a frown.

There's a box of old photos,
At the end of Mum's bed,
And when I look at them,
Happy memories come into my head.

Although we're apart,
We're still all together,
Even if have two families
I'll love them forever.

Coco Boyd Ratcliffe (12)
St Mary's School, Colchester

Waiting At The Bus Stop

It's a crisp October morning,
Many a day, she has seen here dawning,
Waiting at the bus stop.

She never moves an inch,
She's never been seen to flinch,
Waiting at the bus stop.

She shivers in the winter,
She boils in the summer,
Waiting at the bus stop.

Everybody in the town, has seen her,
Everybody wonders her story,
Waiting at the bus stop.

She herself wonders why she stands here,
Waiting, watching, wondering,
Waiting at the bus stop.

Many buses pass,
Still she moves no more,
She is only waiting for the bus that will take her
To death's door.

Helen Pannell (15)
St Mary's School, Colchester

Friends

Friends are like seasons,
They come and sometimes go.

Friends are like flowers,
Sometimes they blossom into your life or they die.

Friends are like the last square of chocolate,
You want to save it, so it lasts forever
Or you want to eat it to get rid of the temptations of going back.

Friends are like apples on an apple tree,
Some stay, some fall.

Friends are like the weather,
They can warm to you or sometimes be frosty.

Friends are like bags and shoes,
You can never have too many.

Friends . . .
Friends are for life.

Maddie Sims (14)
St Mary's School, Colchester

Autumn

Balmy summer days and nights have faded
Away to leave a crisp, empty chill in
The air. The trees appear snug in their cloaks
Of burnt ambers, tawny oranges and
Fantastic crimsons in a marvellous
Show of colour to ensure that we do
Not yearn for the warmth from the absent sun.

The leaves gradually flit and dart in a graceful descent
To weave a thick carpet on the ground
Where the *crunch, crunch, crunch* of feet can be
Heard throughout the day. But soon the leaves will
Disappear and the rich hues of autumn
Are replaced by the bareness of winter
As nature prepares to enter slumber.

Ellen Gage (15)
St Mary's School, Colchester

Individuality

Individuality
Is a word
That's talked about
And often heard.

We all own it
In our own little way
It's almost like a game we play.

Just because I have big, blonde hair
Just because I'm loud out there
Doesn't mean I am not kind
Doesn't mean I do not mind.

It's my individuality
My play in the game
My time to shine
Yes
You take the blame.

Libby Mead (12)
St Mary's School, Colchester

Lifetime

Life is like a ticking clock,
A steady beat that never stops.

Tick tock, tick tock, time is slipping away.

Life may seem to fly on past,
But if you stopped, and made it last . . .

Tick tock, tick tock, time is slipping away.

People come and people go,
But without them time would go more slow.

Tick tock, tick tock, time is slipping away.

But soon the time left is small,
And beyond the grave the voices call.

Tick tock, tick . . . the clock has stopped.

Rebecca Ennion (14)
St Mary's School, Colchester

Is It Too Late?

Is it too late to turn back time?
If we stop now it might be fine.

Causing pollution by over driving,
We don't realise but we are eco skiving.

Cutting down trees and wasting paper,
Don't we think about what's coming later?

Innocent animals cry for help
As we destroy their homes, they let out a yelp.

Leaving taps running and lights switched on,
People think it's all just a con.

What do we do when trouble starts?
Sea levels rising to the top of the charts.

Oh . . . how I wish we could just turn back time!
Instead of ignoring the fact it was bad.
Redo it properly and then be glad!

Joanne Illidge (13)
St Mary's School, Colchester

Reflections

We all worry,
Worry about the view,
The main feature of ourselves,
To match the things we do,
Each and every day,
I guarantee to you,
That you will look in the mirror,
And really hate the view.

Some people feel,
And others just deny,
Some people look away and sigh
Concealer, blusher, bronzer, *wow!*
I look at all their faces, *pow!*
Maybe we can change the scene
It makes me feel so pale and green,
I cannot take it anymore,
I'm leaving . . . leaving … leaving!

Bryony Fenn (13)
St Mary's School, Colchester

Daddy

Someone once told me that every dog has their day.

March 5th he came and went away
A shoulder to cry on, it was always there
Forever and ever but I was still scared
Reminiscing about the days of my early youth
One day you were there, the next you were gone
Forever is hope and hope is forever
Love and cherish and we're all together
I hope for one more goodnight kiss
All the love and the bliss goes for my sis'
You know I miss you, I don't mean to diss you
But you were hardly the best dad in my life
I don't know why, it just makes me wanna cry
I've got to tell the truth 'cause I don't wanna lie
In a way it's my fault
I could've told someone I wanted to see you
So much time, it went past
All those years, they went so fast
All those memories, they never do last
I've got a story, a story that needs to be told
Pass it down, even when I'm old
Pass it down and say, 'Let the good times roll.'
I was there at your funeral; it was stated
Jason Squire has just been cremated
I've cried and cried but no matter
'Cause I want you to know how I feel
When you went six feet under
My head was like thunder
I couldn't think what to say
All I've done every day is sit and pray
Pray that you'll come back some day
You were my sun, my sky
I wish I had a chance to say goodbye.

Reece Squire (14)
The Alec Hunter Humanities College

A True Teenager

'We are the teens of 21st century!'
'A new type' we can be described,
'We are the future,'
A future that is dread.

But the reason for the despair,
Is crime by teens everywhere.
'When will it end?'
I ask myself.

'When can we express our true self?'
The true self that isn't 'violent . . .
Or depressed,
The true self that doesn't require respect.

Respect which some try to achieve with a gun
Bang!
Then there is no one to respect
But can you call it respect
Or a confused mind of a teen
Who is trying too hard?

The true teenager who I am,
Is the one who loves progress . . .
And fun.
Yet knows when to end.
A teenager who wants to grow up
But truly wants to be young.
A teenager who wants to love,
Make peace and be loved
And that is who I am.
So, maybe the world would be a better place,
If everyone could be a real teen again?

Ivan Shipulin (14)
The Alec Hunter Humanities College

Do You Remember

We used to be so free, we could do as we wanted,
The smell of fresh air was so sweet, as we rolled down the bouncy hills.
Do you remember when you took my hand, and made me promise
That things will never change? And I took your hand too and made you promise the same.
But look at us now, I'm standing here and you're over there.
What happened to our promise? Why did we change?
You swear and curse at all the teachers, I laugh at things that aren't funny.
You smoke and do drugs and drink alcohol, and I cover my face with make-up.
You're part of a dangerous gang now and I go to all the night raves.
Yeah, and now we don't even talk much,
You've got your friends and I've got mine.
But that day when you walked past me,
Your eyes, met with my distant gaze.
And for that one moment I wanted to cry,
So much I wanted to go back to those days when I was nine.
And you felt the same - I could tell by your eyes,
They couldn't lie - you wanted to cry too.
So it's true, just like me, you didn't want to forget.
Tears tumbling uncontrollably down my cheeks.
You didn't forget the memory,
You remembered, you remembered too.

Ekenna Oji (14)
The Alec Hunter Humanities College

Only Because I . . .

Just because I do my work, it doesn't mean I am a nerd,
Just because I don't see some of my mates
It doesn't mean I have no friends.
I am what I want to be not what everyone wants me to be
And the only reason I like school is because I want to do something with my life
Not like some people who just end up in a dead end job
And think school is a laugh
And they would get a good job no matter what!
But that's not how it works.
Some people take the mick out of me because I look different
And because they just do it for fun
And they think they are cool when they are not
That is what they think.
Because I don't smoke or take drugs
It doesn't mean I'm not cool in my own way,
I like school but it does not mean I am a nerd,
I am just me, I am what I want to be
And if people don't like it they can say nothing
They don't have to be my mates.

Christine Nelson (13)
The Alec Hunter Humanities College

I'm A Child

I am a child, I like to run,
I am a child, it's really fun,
I get bullied, it's not great,
But it seems to be my fate.

When the day has come to an end,
I really wish I had a friend,
But then I realised I was wrong,
I had loads of friends all along.

I am a child.

Martyn Richardson (12)
The Alec Hunter Humanities College

Untitled

I treat everyone fairly,
I like to look good but I'm not obsessed with looks,
I don't like to litter,
I don't like to swear,
I don't like to be bitter,
I care for others,
I don't break the rules,
Just because I'm a good person you think I'm uncool,
I'm clever, I like lessons,
So apparently I'm a nerd,
Listen up 'cause I really don't care,
I have good friends who will always be there,
I am not perfect at everything but I do like to try,
Just to end I have to say,
I just think you're horrible which somehow makes you cool
Just ask yourself who will be there at the end of the day?

Hope Dodge (11)
The Alec Hunter Humanities College

Grandad, My Poem To You

Everywhere I turn I'm thinking of you
But there's nothing I can say to change the past
I'd do anything with my power
I'd give everything I've got
Just to bring you back, back to me.

I know you want me to be free and happy,
But without you I can't do it, I need you
I can't see another way
And I can't face another day without you.

Please come back and bring a smile on my face
With your eyes of brown
And your heart of gold.

I miss you Grandad.

Laura Wiffen (14)
The Alec Hunter Humanities College

Teenage Life Is Kinda Cool

My life is rubbish
I get blamed for everything
Turn off the telly, tidy up your room, stop complaining
You wouldn't like to be me, honestly.

My life is a dump
I want to throw it in the bin

Some people bully me
It's not my fault that I'm made to be

My life sucks
I'm like a flea

But I'm liking myself now
And I'm not gonna fib.

Emily Bunyan (11)
The Alec Hunter Humanities College

Compliments

If you're a negative person,
You find them in lots of places,
If you're given a compliment,
Why throw it back in their faces?

You could say
Thank you, cheers, thanks or ta,
You wouldn't refuse it if it was a gift,
Would you refuse a spanking new car?

You wouldn't cos it's valuable
And compliments don't have value.
No, no way! Wrong!
They thought of nice things to say to you.

So if you're a negative person
This is what to do,
When you receive a compliment, just say,
'Thank you.'

Rhiannon Garrard (12)
The Boswells School

Alone

The way he swaggers as he walks past me,
So confident with shine, people can see.
Gleaming big blue eyes, chocolate-brown hair,
Relaxed in his zone, he just doesn't care!

Smart and intelligent with all his brains,
No effort is needed, to watch it pains!
Girls running over to see what he's got,
Boys watching, then waiting, 'He's not that hot!'

He's not only fit, he's good at all sport.
When other lads ask he says he's self-taught!
Cheerleaders waiting, just for him to score,
Looking so good it has to be the law.

All those pretty girls, they all have a chance,
All with good figures, can sing and can dance!
Perfect clear skin, gorgeous hair, sparkling smile.
My hair just hangs, I've had braces a while!

Valentine's is coming, I start to dread.
I know in my heart and inside my head.
He is the one that is perfect right now.
Attention is needed, I don't know how!

I do not want him just for his good looks.
Not for his money or for what he cooks.
I want to get to know him, maybe more,
Not for what other girls want him for!

All that I ask is for one great big chance,
Maybe I can learn to sing and dance!
A bit of confidence for him to see,
So on Feb the fourteenth, I'm not lonely!

Hollie Robinson (14)
The Sweyne Park School

Achievement

Special badges,
Gold forms,
Letters home that inform,
My parents that I've done good,
And that in class I've understood.

Achievement can mean anything,
From writing a good song to sing,
To winning an important match,
Or helping Mr Garrod's veggie patch.

Going on special trips,
Or drawing great comic strips,
School council, E-mentors too,
Representing our school in blue!

Earning lots and lots of As,
For doing well in my essays,
In Food cooking eggs in a frying pan
Or Mr Woods saying that, 'You're the man!'

Doing well in my French test,
With teachers helping me to be the best,
Sporting excellence, it is so great,
In English winning a big debate.

Wanting to do well in my GCSEs
Lots of A stars – oh yes please,
I want to achieve in future days,
Let's hope my hard work really pays.

Daniel Waggon (13)
The Sweyne Park School

Heroes

H ooray our army's coming home
E veryone is a hero
R eally cool and brave
O ur soldiers are all heroes.

Andrew Dartnell (12)
The Sweyne Park School

Heroes Aren't Brave

Heroes aren't brave,
Heroes aren't bold,
Heroes don't have to be
Young, they can be old.

Heroes aren't fierce,
Heroes aren't tough,
Heroes can be smart and neat,
Instead of being rough.

But heroes are great,
Saviour of the day,
But when their time is done,
They just fade away.

A hero doesn't have to be Superman,
Fly with his cape,
Heroes aren't like those heroes,
Until they awake.

Looking for life's problems,
For a long, long time,
Thinking about them hard,
From sundown to sunshine.

Heroes will take action,
He'll be saviour of the day,
But when his time comes,
He will just fade away.

Jason Keys (13)
The Sweyne Park School

Grendel

His melted eyes dripping messily
His disgusting teeth grinding nastily
His sharp claws ripping angrily
His jagged scales breaking quickly
His rotting tail waving madly
His black heart bleeding furiously.

Daniel Moore (11)
The Sweyne Park School

Beowulf

Beowulf from a faraway land,
A wealthy warrior, so strong and so tall.
His bright blue eyes
With his blue coat under a silver mail shirt.

He travels to Heorot, to defeat the Grendel
The bone-crunching, limb-tearing monster,
Who walks this Earth,
As a threat to the people.
Snatching sleepers from their beds,
Where they are peacefully dreaming.

Beowulf kills the monster,
That comes one night.
Grendel greedily looks at his prey
And then is surprised,
By Beowulf's mortal strength.
But now it is all too late.
For the monster is forced,
To rip off his own limp arm.

The evil monster struggles back to his swamp home,
But in a matter of hours he is dead.

So Beowulf is the hero,
Who saved the people of Heorot.
Who now may live the rest of their lives in peace.

Kai McKechnie (12)
The Sweyne Park School

The Grendel

Poisonous eyes glowing deadly
Sharp teeth, dripping ferociously
Razor claws ripping madly
Slimy scales tensing rapidly
Injured arm bleeding badly
Endless tail trailing roughly
Evil heart planning wickedly.

Aaron Jones (11)
The Sweyne Park School

Beowulf Poem

He came out of the shadows,
His eyes blue and shiny bright.
He wore a dark blue cloak and helmet,
Oh, what a wonderful sight!
Through the shadows I could see
That this strange man in front of me,
Held a sword in one big hand,
And a jewel-encrusted shield that was grand!
Oh, what a wonderful sight that night,
That strange man who came to me,
His angelic fair hair and muscles a-bare,
He kneeled in front of me,
And I trembled in his wake.
For now he spoke in soft and quiet words,
That I had to strain to listen,
This was quite absurd.
He said, 'I have travelled many seas,
To treat your terrible woes,
For wherever evil seeks me, I
Beowulf will go.'
His golden aura surrounded his head,
I thought this was my chance,
To rid my land of evil and terror,
And to have the final dance.

Olivia Unwin (11)
The Sweyne Park School

The Grendel

Blue eyes shining sharply.
Scared teeth biting dangerously.
Brown claws clawing slowly.
Green scales gleaming magically.
Hairy arms bruising quickly.
Bent tail moving fiercely.
Frozen heart beating rapidly.

Freddie Bentley (12)
The Sweyne Park School

I Have A Dream

I have a dream of the world,
I wish it was a clean, clean world,
A kind and beautiful world,

I have a dream of a crimeless world,
No knife crime and No gun crime world,
In fact a good, good world,

I have a dream of a friendly world,
A kind and healthy world,
A happy and non-polluted world,

I have a dream of no racism,
Of the whole world,
In fact a non-violent world,
With no wars at all,

In all the world,
I'd love to say that,
All of the world should,
Have peace someday.

Michael Bewers (11)
The Sweyne Park School

The Sea

The sea, the sea, the sea is blue,
The sea, the sea, the sea is you,
The sea, the sea, a watery domain,
The sea, the sea bears an insufferable pain.

The sea, the sea carries plenty of boats,
The sea, the sea is cold so wear a coat,
The sea, the sea has plenty of fish,
But fish is nice eaten on a dish.

The waves, the waves smash with all their might,
The waves, the waves, they crash with all their bite,
The waves, the waves are the kings,
The waves, the waves are carried by the wind.

Bradley Keys (12)
The Sweyne Park School

The Loch Ness Monster

While the sunlight could still be seen
He waits beneath the shadows
Disguised by scales of dark green
He can still remember when he was free
Far from all of human kind
Now watched every minute of the hour
Left without any freedom nor power
Leaving his peculiar past behind
Only to be watched by undiverted eyes
Men sitting by the loch
Whispering mysterious tales and lies
And mythical trails of where he had once been
Or were his species used to deem
Laughing and listening as the humans mock
He exist unexploited in the murky loch.

Jessica Sterling (13)
The Sweyne Park School

Thanks Miss!

Miss, I decided to write you a poem,
And this time it will not rhyme, as poems do
Not have to rhyme.
You are cool, C,'double O, L' (note the quote from AIC!)
You're like a Malteser, hard on the outside
But light and bubbly on the inside.
You have ruled us like 'Ralph', I feared you like 'the beast'
However you are not scary, I see that now
Thanks to that 'light from yonder window'.
It will now 'take more than a tangible ghost to frighten me'.
I'm quite proud, I've used quotes from every text we've studied in literature.
I've also used caesuras, semi-colons, and enjambment. Be impressed!
However, I fear that there are internal rhymes, so, this is actually an epic failure.
All the best and thanks for everything!

Rachel Hudson (16)
The Sweyne Park School

Our Heroes

'The war to end all wars,'
Or so every person thought,
One man's passion, another man's bloodlust,
We respect you, our heroes,
You vulnerable, naïve, brave boys,
And the loves you left behind.
Without you, we wouldn't be us,
Your death, our life,
Thank you is not enough,
Forever is not enough,
To mend the wounds and breaks and scars the war left on us.
But we will always remember you,
The world will always remember you,
Our heroes, our true, misguided heroes.

Alice Hodkinson (15)
The Sweyne Park School

The Winning Loser

A loser is a winner really,
The one who tries again,
With courage, strength and wisdom,
Tenacity and game.

After many failures,
He once insists again,
After being battered,
He tries, mentally in pain.

He has experience,
Being used like a spinner,
Going round and round,
But is transformed into a winner.

Harry Ludlow (15)
The Sweyne Park School

What Makes A Hero?

A hero is brave,
A hero is understanding,
A hero is mysterious,
Who is your hero?

A hero is caring,
A hero is always there for you,
A hero is kind,
Where is your hero?

A hero is helpful,
A hero is generous,
A hero is selfless,
So what makes your hero?

George Barker (13)
The Sweyne Park School

Death

Death is a force an inescapable grasp,
Who knows how long this old man will last?
He can hear Death's call, he can hear the bells ring,
That deafening noise, *ring-a-ding-ding*.
Sirens calling for him in the cold dust of night,
That mystifying, law-defying non-denying light.
It is now almost time to take his last days,
It's coming closer, his life he pays.
Death's touch is the electrifying buzz,
Get that feeling in your body and giant fuzz.
His time is upon us time to take a flight,
'Take me, take me, take me away into the night.'

Connor Thompson (12)
The Sweyne Park School

A Hero

A hero is someone with a secret identity,
A hero is someone who saves a person like you or me.

A hero can be just as simple as your own mum and dad,
For me, my family are the best heroes I've ever had.

Some people say police are heroes for a laugh,
And all those dog homes make sure their animals don't starve.

A hero is someone who helps you when you're in trouble,
They can especially help you when you get in a bit of a muddle.

A hero can come in many shapes and sizes you see,
But underneath it all, the real heroes are you and me.

Gemma Gilson (12)
The Sweyne Park School

Firefighter

F ire and fighting are her magical powers
I nitialising data that's clues to the mysteries
R escuing people is her job
E nduring the most life-threatening dangers and situations
F ighting is her way of winning
I nterrogating people, she does a lot
G reat and kind-hearted, she is
H elps lots of people day and night
T rashing away the bad deeds
E very day she is called upon
R ising her ability all the time.

Shauna Quinn (11)
The Sweyne Park School

I Love To Dance

I love to dance
I always go to a hall
I gave my boyfriend one more chance
So he took me to the mall!

Megan Leighton (13)
The Sweyne Park School

I Love You!

I n the night I think about you

L ove is for people to live in harmony
O ut of all of them, I love you the most
V ery precious to me
E very day I feel as if you are in my arms

Y ou're the only one I love
O h you are so handsome
U nder my skin, I love you the most.

Charlotte Mayo (11)
The Sweyne Park School

My Hero

My hero is fast
My hero is strong
My hero plays for Arsenal
My hero is Fabregas.

My hero can sing
My hero can rap
My hero is a legend
My hero is Eminem.

David Greenslade (12)
The Sweyne Park School

The Grendel

Bloodshot eyes staring suspiciously
Sharp teeth grinding hatefully
Pointed claws ripping carelessly
Slimy scales bleeding strangely
Scarred arm grabbing wildly
Hairy tail wagging uncontrollably
Cold heart beating faintly.

George Izod (11)
The Sweyne Park School

Dedication To My Sister

As all the seasons pass us by,
I know that Bethany will always fly.

Like a butterfly gliding high,
I know that she will always be mine.

Bethany will perch on a white lily,
I know that she will always be free.

Georgina Davis (11)
The Sweyne Park School

Leaves – Haiku

Oh the leaves are dead
There is colour in the leaves
Different sizes.

Mitchell Lambe (12)
The Sweyne Park School

Happiness

My happiness is a hot sun shining down brightly on the world below.
The sharp lemon-yellow turns softly to fresh snow-white
As it drifts slowly down.
Through the window of the grey, dark classroom,
Shines a beam of light, a ray of hope to the children,
Telling them there is a way of escaping.

It shines down on the jungle, breaking the cold night air.
It wakes the animals from their deepest dreams.

It shines down, burning through the ice.
The polar bear knows it's time to show her little cubs the outside world,
When the water gathers around her paws.
It's time for her to quench her thirst
And enjoy her first meal for months.

My happiness is a hot sun
It allows me to live and makes my life a whole lot better!

Jessica Rowe (13)
Thurstable School

Bruised

My name is Chloe; I am five years old,
I go to school, I am in Year 1.
I get up at 6 o'clock,
Get myself ready and make breakfast,
I go round the house, make sure it's tidy,
Make myself look perfect for her to see.
She stumbles downstairs with a bottle of wine,
Her words are slurred as she shouts, 'Get going!'
I stop and stare at my monster of a mum,
She grabs my arm as I close my eyes.
Twenty constant pains rush beneath my skin.
I fall to the ground as I'm kicked out of the house.
I pick myself up, brush myself down.
Now I'm ready to face the world.
As I stroll through the cold December day,
The tears prick my eyes and begin to trickle.
The day rolls by so quickly,
I'm lost in this trance of what she'll do next,
When I walk through the door my life's crazy mess.
As soon as I step through the door,
She's standing there, eyes narrowed towards me.
Her arms crossed over her chest,
My heart leaps straight into my mouth.
My face goes drained and cold,
My hands begin to sweat and clam up.
What have I done this time? I think,
As I drop my bag onto the floor.
She takes a few steps towards me,
She says I didn't do good enough job.
The anger in her eyes make me shiver with fright,
She drags me to the lounge by my collar.
And throws me in a heap on the floor,
My body feels shattered, broken to pieces . . .

Charlotte Hood (12)
Thurstable School

The Bell Rings

The bell rings in the morning
Children come flooding in
People trudging to lesson one
In the light of the yellow sun

The bell rings in the morning
Lesson two begins
People working noisily
Adding the square of two.

The bell rings in the morning
Lesson three begins
People moving to lesson three
Learning the German word for tree.

The bell rings in the morning
Lesson four begins
The sun gleams on the window
The computer crashes again.

The bell rings in the morning
Lesson five begins
Children misbehaving
Writing a poem about school.

The bell rings in the morning
The buses line up in a road
Everyone rushing home
Bus cards on the floor.

The bell rings in the morning
Not a sound is heard
Empty, desolate and quiet
Not a soul in sight.

The bell rings in the morning
Another day begins . . .

Toby Price (12)
Thurstable School

The Girl . . .

She was just seven when it started,
Even though she knew it wasn't right,
She couldn't tell anyone,
Every time she saw him her face turned white.

She had to go there every Wednesday,
When her mother was at work,
How was she supposed to tell her though?
She would never believe he was such a jerk.

She told her friend one day at school,
And asked if her uncle did the same,
But her teacher overheard the chat,
Assured her she was not to blame.

She told her teacher everything,
But then her teacher called the police,
They later on arrested him,
And asked why he did this to his niece.

But he denied it all,
Said it was not true,
That his niece was lying,
And that was nothing new.

But the police didn't believe him,
Turns out she cried so many tears,
What sick kind of man would do that?
He was locked up for seven years.

The girl was so happy,
He was gone from her life,
She lived the rest of her life happily,
She became a mother of three and a beautiful wife.

Megan House (12)
Thurstable School

My Time At War

The posters at home said it would be good,
The posters at home said that I should.
Join the army, fight for the king,
Keep safe my family till victory bells ring.

I signed the papers, went out to war,
Where I saw dead soldiers upon the floor.
The look of the men, the shots from the gun,
I thought that the posters said this would be fun.

I sat there alone, no good food to eat,
Wondering when we would have Germany beat.
They said just two weeks, it had now been a year,
I thought of my family when I was filled with fear.

The contact from home was a damp, screwed up letter,
The trenches were bad, they should've been much better.
We didn't expect the machine guns at all,
They were what made most of our soldiers fall.

The Germans with gas, oh that was a sight,
That gave all our troops such a terrible fright.
The Germans shot gas, it came in overhead,
If we inhaled the fumes, we would surely be dead.

We got out the masks, put them over our faces,
I could not find mine, I searched many places.
It had gone missing, of what I was sure,
I knew that my life would soon be no more.

A soldier was rotting, I saw him ahead,
I struggled towards him, past all the dead.
I put on his mask, at last I could breathe,
Then back to the dugouts through dead men I weaved.

Rachel Etherington (14)
Thurstable School

A Speck Of Dust

Sometimes I stay awake at night,
And think of who I am,
For I'm am individual,
Who doesn't have a gang.

You may think that I'm nerdy,
A speck of dust to you,
I may be classed as ugly,
I suppose this could be true.

They think that I'm a weakling,
The cool kids they all stare,
They laugh and joke behind my back,
This really isn't fair.

It isn't really physical,
But verbal it could be,
They start to call me horrible names,
I hate it but I see.

I count the days that pass away,
Where I've been left alone,
They've egged my house and put me down
And threatened me on the phone.

I can't say that I'm suicidal,
I really don't want that,
I just wish that they'd stop the names,
Like twonk and snitch and fat.

But now I don't sit upright,
I lay down on my bed,
I put it all behind me,
And think of friends instead.

Elliot Hawkins (12)
Thurstable School

My Dream

I felt so near
The goal very near
My ambitious dream
Not as far as it seemed.

I stepped up to the block
I could see the clock
My heart beat quick
I would really have to kick.

The turn was good
But not as well as I could
I kicked and kicked as the clock ticked
My dream really could not be nicked.

My lungs would burst
The finish a thirst
I lunged for the pad
I must have taken it by a tad.

I twisted my neck
Just to check
I didn't have to win it
Just wanted to go under one minute
Please let it be
Yes – 59.63!

I jumped for joy
Like a wind up toy
I saluted the crowd
My coach was proud.

Sonny Trigg (13)
Thurstable School

A Change Overnight

All these happy memories,
Of the people he loves,
Fading from his mind,
As they slip away.

The painful ones,
Which we spent together,
I know it happened,
But we won't remember.

No longer the past,
Only the future
He remembers the lights,
Then a massive crash.

I wait by his bed,
For his eyes to open,
And the words to come out,
'What happened?'

The yellow light,
But a sudden bright light,
Fading slowly,
To the pitch-black dark.

The accident last night
So unplanned and a shock,
That last night was . . .
A car crash, which changed his life.

Rebecca Lockwood (13)
Thurstable School

Hallowe'en

Hallow'een is on the 31st October
Hallowe'en is a dark night
Hallowe'en is a night of frights and scares
Hallowe'en is a night of lit-up faces
Of pumpkins glowing in the darkness of the night
Hallowe'en is a night of scary costumes and faces.

Amy Dignum (11)
Thurstable School

I'm Just That Kinda Girl

They say we are these silly girls
Who always mess around,
The ones who'll stand out in the rain,
Or roll across the ground.

They say we are those silly girls
The 'weirdos' you might name,
Who'll shout out random words in class,
You think we're quite insane.

But really we're those kind of girls
Who aren't afraid of fun,
Who are not afraid to get wet hair,
Or to get a muddy bum!

Cos really we're those kind of girls
Who know one life, one chance,
Who know to have fun whilst they can,
Who'll join in every dance.

We'll be those grannies in the home
Who'll race around on chairs,
Who'll grab a mattress off a bed,
And ride it down the stairs!

I am who I am,
I'll do what I'll do,
And that's the way I'll
Always be.

Heather Acketts (12)
Thurstable School

Blue

Blue is the sea moving slowly in the breeze.
Blue is the sky shining down.
Blue is the school door opening and closing.
Blue is Molly's dog barking and barking.
Blue is Holly's pen writing and writing all day long
Blue is a colour just sitting next to you.

Jodie Haertel (11)
Thurstable School

It Won't Stop

They yelled at me,
Now I'm crying,
They screamed at me for nothing,
Now I'm crying,
I let out a scream,
Now I'm crying.

They told me not to yell,
I feel I'm dying.
They won't stop,
I feel I'm dying.
I need to tell,
I feel I'm dying.

They hit out,
I hid under my bed.
They punched,
I hid under my bed.
They started to shout,
I hid under my bed.

I'm in pain,
It's gone to my head,
I can't go out,
It's gone to my head,
I've gone insane,
It's gone to my head.

Heidi Sale (12)
Thurstable School

My Anger Is . . .

My anger is a fiery river,
Burning specks of joy in its path
Flowing deep inside,
Scattering blood-curdling flames,
The bubbling lava covers a pool of cool serenity.
Screaming out a song of pain.
Raging terror as dark as the inside of a train tunnel.

Elizabeth David (13)
Thurstable School

You Are My BFF!

I know today we argued,
And what I'm saying is true,
You are my BFF
So I want to make it up to you.

You know that she spreads rumours,
So please believe me only,
I couldn't live without you,
I would be so lonely,

You're always there for me,
And you've never turned away,
I hope we stay friends forever,
No matter what they say,

We've had our little arguments,
Nearly everybody does,
Problems never last for long,
With unique friends like us,

Thanks for being there for me,
Our friendship's strong and true,
And I just want to let you know,
I'm always there for you!

Katie Smart (13)
Thurstable School

My Jealousy

My jealousy is an unforgiving iceberg.
It sits with its back to all, lonely in its silent blue lake.
It is cold and unchanged, unforgiving.
It watches and despises with an ugly green aura hanging around it.
Many avoid it, knowing its cold and icy heart has no emotions or feelings;
Just the quiet stare of glassy eyes.

My jealousy is an iceberg
But melts away after time collapses it
Into the swirling pool of emotions
Where it began.

Callum Hultquist (13)
Thurstable School

The Tears Of A Planet

The world is in a delicate state,
We don't know if it's too late,
The climate is changing, people are told,
The Earth is ill but it's more than a cold.

Water levels rising, higher and higher,
The flood barriers are starting to tire,
People neglecting it, people trying to say,
'Not for much longer, we'll keep it at bay.'

The ozone layer not fully made,
Soon the pollution will fade,
Animals and people and plants as well,
Will be taken over by watery hell.

Planets alone, no human life,
No pollution, no cars, no strife,
Earth will be fine without us here,
A ball of water, a big tear.

We must do something for the Earth's sake,
Turn off the TV, have a computer break,
Anything that will help the world's cause,
Heal its pain, heal its sores.

Jamie David Allen (13)
Thurstable School

Caused By My Tears

They all say I'm ugly, they call me a nerd,
I can't take it any longer, they call me mean words.

I sit up all night and think, *what have I done?*
I sit there and say, that I have done nothing wrong.

I stood up to my bullies,
They all had to mention,
I started a fight, and got an hour's detention.

The bullying was over, so I went home for tea,
There sat my mum, disappointed in me.

Charley Bowhill (12)
Thurstable School

Blighty

I love old Blighty;
During the winter;
It's warmer up in Scotland than Cornwall,
Rain, snow, cloudy.

I love old Blighty;
During the spring,
Our pretty daisies flower;
Little lambs are here.

I love old Blighty;
During the summer,
Hand held fans, fish and chips;
Temperature past 10 degrees, beaches are full.

I love old Blighty;
During the autumn;
Orange, brown, beige leaves skip the paths;
The smell of harvested crops fills the air.

I do love old Blighty,
I really do,
But I prefer the Caribbean,
It's warmer there.

Billy Martyn (11)
Thurstable School

School

School is boring,
I am always snoring,
My mum keeps phoning,
And the teacher is moaning,
I need some food,
Because I'm in a bad mood,
Lots of tests,
Sleeping on the desk,
I am feeling very bright,
Then I have a fight!

Charlie Flanagan(11)
Thurstable School

It

It wasn't just a picture,
It was another world,
Another universe,
Lines that flowed and curled.

Jagged lines and circles,
Something new at every glance,
A fairy tale, a tricky map,
A knight, a children's dance.

Splashes of colour,
Patches of light,
Dark in the middle,
Reminds me of night.

All woven together,
A story of sorts,
A portrait of a princess?
Or a witch with hairy warts?

A paintbrush moves across the wall,
It magics up the new,
We all see something different here,
In red and green and blue.

Mary-Ann Anthony (13)
Thurstable School

My Family

Mums can moan, their voices like thunder
Dads can be a drag,
Like toilet roll stuck to your foot.
Nans can nag, their voices like a dog's bark.
Grandads can be grumpy
Like when their porridge goes lumpy.
But no matter what happens,
You always are loved.
You can't choose your family,
No matter what.

Kelsey Graham (11)
Thurstable School

Always Waiting

Great, late again, I hope he's not there,
French, the one lesson I have with him,
I enter C block, the air stifled with fear,
I know he's waiting, he's always waiting.

Inhaling dust and cigarette butts
The teachers flouting what they proclaim,
Frightfully trembling in I bustle past,
I know he's waiting, he's always waiting.

Looking around, no glisten, disgust,
A poor excuse for a mundane school,
The door flings open, a figure appears,
I know he's waiting, I can see him waiting.

The register's called, imposing order,
His face is the pinnacle of hate,
Hope amongst it seldom to be seen,
He's coming at me, the wait is over.

He'd lunge at me, one more to my chest,
No bastion to save me, no protection,
My money taken, one less lunch to delve in,
Yet no more waiting, no more waiting.

William Pryke (13)
Thurstable School

Black

Black is a dark colour waiting to be found,
Black is an evil colour waiting and waiting until night,
Black is a scary colour unleashed at night,
Black is a monster in my wardrobe,
Black are the deep, luminous, red eyes under my bed,
Black is the shadow casting over my bed,
Black is the colour that dyes my walls,
Black is a colour which vaporises in sunlight,
Black is no more until night,
Black is death.

Kester Reeve (11)
Thurstable School

Broken

I am alone, I have no family,
I have no friends, I am alone.
I have a home. Well, not a real home anyway.
As I lay in my bed resting my sorrowed head.
I feel a hole in my heart, my life has been torn apart.
Why doesn't anybody care?
As I stand there in silence and try to talk to my peers,
They ignore me and I break down in tears.
But then I come home, and I already feel a fist,
Before it's even brushed against my skin.
I hear a creak, it's *him*.
My heart starts pounding,
I feel as if I'm about to swallow my stomach,
I start breathing heavier, heavier and heavier.
'You're late,' he whispers.
'Sorry erm, erm.' I pause.
I see him clench his hard, stone-cold fists.
I count to myself: '5, 4, 3,2, 1.'
He goes repeating his actions again.
He grabs me
I'll leave the rest to your imagination.

Ellie-Jane Oliver (12)
Thurstable School

Sunset

Orange is a warm summery sunset
Hiding behind the horizon.
The sun is hiding,
He is playing a game with the moon!

Summer has three friends,
Winter, autumn and spring.

Spring has a warm sunset
But not as hot as the summer sun.

Winter has a cold sun
The coldest sun like no other.

Charlotte Leavett-Shove (11)
Thurstable School

Nobody Said

Laughter and hatred,
Sinister, sly,
Evil and nasty,
All a big lie.

'You little nerd,'
'You are such a teacher's pet.'
They enjoy, I bet.

Sitting in a corner,
Cramped and scared,
Waiting for it to happen,
As the bullies stared.

Too much anger,
Too many rumours spread,
Of lying and cheating,
That's all I said.

Now it's all over,
It was all in my head,
All the hatred and evil,
Nobody said.

Joss Saunders (12)
Thurstable School

The Rain Cloud

As the cloud floats in the sky,
High, high, high.
His friends start to laugh
They're laughing because the cloud is small,
Unlike them all.

The cloud is sad, it's flying away,
Into all the dark clouds.
It must be scared because it feels all swollen.
Water slowly starts to drop.
'What is happening to me?
Oh no, I have turned into a rain cloud.'

Katie Wollington (11)
Thurstable School

Just Maybe

I never thought it would get this far,
But now it's just not funny
They laugh at me and call me names
And never seem to care
It seems like I'm a joke
The one who they can push around
They snatch my bag
And take my shoes
It seems like I'm a game
The one who always loses
When they beat me up
My heart seems to skip a beat
It seems like she's a giant
I'm always looking up at her
She bosses me around
And tells me I'm a loser
But maybe
Just maybe
I am cool
I am pretty!

Georgia Kyne (12)
Thurstable School

Nature

I am free,
Swaying in a tree.
Running through the field,
Never to yield.
I am flying high,
In the deep blue sky.
Clouds like a cushion
One big illusion.
Fighting through the dark,
With just one bright spark.
Just that I am in a dream,
Never to be seen.

Ellen Trollope (11)
Thurstable School

I Will Stand By You

Friends are trustworthy,
They stand by you.
Friends are encouraging,
They understand everything you do.
Friends are people you can trust,
Tell all your secrets to.
If I was your friend,
I would cherish everything you do.
Friends are like family,
Close to your heart.
I would respect them,
Straight from the start.
I have many friends,
We are one big team.
They are reliable and honest,
They are all kind to me.
If you are someone,
Who is always alone.
Make many friends,
Don't sit back and moan.

Charleigh Green (12)
Thurstable School

The Lion

The beauty of the jungle
With its long orange tail
Its bright yellow eyes
It will make you look like a snail
With its speed and height
Faster than light
And its fiery mane
And its clever brain
To catch his prey
You might just find
To go near this creature
You're out of your mind.

Gemma Bird (13)
Thurstable School

Untitled

Summer has three friends, Winter, Autumn and Spring,
Who all like to play different things.

Winter likes to run all wrapped up warm
    Scarves
        Hats
            Gloves.

Autumn never plays, just gets blown in the wind.
    Swish,
        Swish
            Swish.

Spring likes to play find the egg,
When the baby animals arrive.
    Moo
        Baa
            Baa
                Oink.

But summer doesn't know what to play,
So he lies on his back all day!

Katy Rose Payne (11)
Thurstable School

Misery

My misery is a murderous iceberg crushing anything in its path
Not thinking about the consequences.
Down goes the Titanic but I stay afloat,
A cold polar-hearted miserable nothing on a sea of dreams drifting forever.
People only see my exterior underneath the depths
I'm a giant icy boulder of distress.

The winter of despair continues through the endless night
Until the dawn of happiness banishes the darkness to the deeper corners of Hell
And fire up the furnaces of joy.
Then when the bright warm sun comes and heats up this ship of despair,
The ice cracks, a heart beats and I'm happy again.

Robert James Gill (13)
Thurstable School

Dark Eclipse

My anger is a dark eclipse,
Shadowing the world,
Shrouding everyone in fury.
The ground squeaks with fear,
The mountains rumble with anxiety,
My anger is everything.

My anger is a dark eclipse,
Filling everything with darkness,
And for those few moments,
It is I; not anyone or anything else
That the world fears.
My anger is everything.

My anger is a dark eclipse,
But eclipses soon come to an end,
So that my moment of anger is forgotten
And the Earth is still,
The mountains quiet.
My anger was everything.

Daisy Smith (13)
Thurstable School

Anger

My anger is a fiery volcano,
Exploding loudly within the jungle.
Hot lava pours down the mountainside
As people running scream for survival.
Buildings shake before crashing to the ground.
While clouds of smoke fill the air covering the once-blue skies.
I stand watching as destruction fills the city.

Little children run to their mothers,
Into their arms full of love and protection.
Animals flee from the place they call home,
Into the danger of the fiery volcano.
But hope will come as sirens blare,
To save the people from my anger.

Emme Ross (13)
Thurstable School

Swirl

I am a swirl,
Spinning round and round,
Making you dizzy
Till you fall to the ground.

I am a colour,
Every colour in the world,
Dull and bright,
Dark and light.

I am happy,
Happy as can be,
Making you happy,
Happy as me.

I am excitement
Jumping around
Never letting your feet,
Touch the ground,

Add it altogether and that makes swirl!

Lucy Greed (11)
Thurstable School

Blue Cows

The blue cow lives in the farmhouse
Perched across the bubblegum tree,
The tree sits in the diamond field.

The field grows purple carrots
They don't grow many because the blue cows steals them all,
They fly very high pointing their big toes out
To sell them at the picky pocky market.

'Quack, quack!' they say at the market doing bargain deals
The clouds are falling to the ground
Crushing the tiny people at the picky pocky market.

So sad now the blue cow has to go home
And eat them all.

Samuel James (11)
Thurstable School

I Am A Splodge

I am a splodge
I live in a painting
Waiting and waiting
Till everyone's gone.

I wait in the daylight
Watching everyone
They stare and stare
And I strike when it's bare.

I am a splodge
My life is in a painting
I see nothing
I am a splodge.

At night when it's empty
The lights are off
Pitch-black . . .
I can see nothing, I am in nothing
No . . . I am in a painting, I am a splodge.

Sonya Zemmiri (11)
Thurstable School

The Big Worm Stole The Sunglasses

The big worm stole the sunglasses,
Even though they don't have eyes.
The big worm stole the sunglasses and showed all his friends.
Out came the birds like German battle planes shooting down.
The big worm stole the sunglasses, bright as the sun shining.
Darkness struck the garden giants walking around
They picked up the glasses and took them to their lap
Well that's what the worms thought.
They scurried quickly to the house.
The giants were on the run with the sunglasses.
The big worm stole the sunglasses, but he didn't have them any more.
Sadness struck the garden, silence of the night,
Peace and quiet.
The big worm stole the sunglasses but didn't have them anymore.

James Johnson (11)
Thurstable School

Footprints

As he tossed a rock towards the sky
He told me I was his final goodbye.
He said he had left me to last
He didn't want time to flow too fast.

As the sun rays shone on the beach
He took me places I would never have reached
As stars would shoot across the sky
His words were like a lullaby.

He said, 'Do not fear when I am far
Because I'm always there within your heart
Explore the world, just always believe
Because there's a life out there when I leave.'

He walked away, he left footprints in the sand
He left me there without a helping hand
As I walked away, to the beach's coast
I thought to myself,
It takes an angel to know a ghost.

Molly-Rose Gosling (13)
Thurstable School

Homework

Homework, a daily chore,
Homework, a terrible bore,
Homework, too much work,
Homework, an annoying berk.
Homework, always there,
Homework, why is it there?
Because every day there's more *homework, homework, homework!*
Homework, so frustrating,
Homework, my anger is escalating,
Homework, at least sometime it will stop,
Homework, for my sake, it definitely has to stop,
Homework, always there
Homework, why is it there?
Because every day there's more *homework, homework, homework!*

Mark Oldham (12)
Thurstable School

My Feelings

My sorrow is a piercing sound,
That damages people's delicate hearing,
It jumps like a mysterious monkey, tree to tree.
My anger is a fiery volcano,
That leaks lava day and night,
It erupts my fire, but then there is silence,
When a cool breeze emerges.
My grief is a hot, sun,
That when people breathe, they breathe in my intense bubbly steam,
That emerges out from the sky.
My love is a breezy promise, it flows down a serene river,
My river does not stop, and neither does love.
My jealousy is a bitter gas, known to be dangerous toxic,
But people can't see it,
Because before they have the chance,
They taste it.
But all my fulfilled feelings have a fulfilled meaning,
And that is for me to know, and you to find out.

Lewis Scrivener (14)
Thurstable School

The Cat

There is a cat
She has white fur
She has a long tail
She has small ears

She has a small nose
She has small eyes
She has long whiskers
She has sharp teeth.

She is a cat
She is a cat
She is a cat
She is a cat

She is a cat!

Thomas Dale (11)
Thurstable School

Sisters

Sisters blame you for things you didn't do,
They always lose your things,
Then get away with, 'Wasn't me, it was you!'

Sisters boss you around,
Demanding you get them this, get them that.
They take your clothes, then throw them to the ground,
Treading on a shoe, tripping on a hat.

Sisters make you feel angry, stupid or sad,
They tell you off, then call you a boff,
But really sisters aren't that bad.

Sisters blame you for things you didn't do,
But all the times you were crying,
They were there for you.

So my sisters and I,
Till the day we die,
Will love each other always.

Charlotte Smith (13)
Thurstable School

Alone

Nobody around except one tree,
Alone, swaying in the breeze,
Gently whispering into the air,
Rustling without a care.
Crunchy leaves fall to the floor,
A family behind a door.
A bird in a nest tweeting in the tree,
Calling out to you and me.
Its mum close, keeping an eye,
Trusting us to help it fly.

Then the day comes to a close
Sorry that we have to go,
See you tomorrow at midday,
Then we can go and play.

Katie Polley (12)
Thurstable School

Bad Habits

It used to happen once a week,
Now it happens all the time.
He made me special,
Like the world was mine.

He'd make me feel unwanted,
But now he makes me feel small.
I used to think he understood me,
Now he never asks how I feel at all.

At first I liked it,
He was my best friend.
Now he's a haunting nightmare,
That never seems to end.

It's like a routine at 6 o'clock,
Here he comes once again creeping on his toes.
He edges over to where I lay,
Bad habits I suppose.

Madeleine Nixson (12)
Thurstable School

My Race

I was in a race
Going at a good pace
I had won
I was the champion
The pool was empty
I didn't get a penalty
I walked up to get my medal
My team mates cheered me on
And I was having fun
I drove back home
And I held my phone
My medal went up to the wall
Then I heard my phone call
I had won
I was the champion!

Dolly Trigg (11)
Thurstable School

Some Friend

I didn't think I did anything,
Obviously she did,
All I did was speak my mind,
As she always would.

I know what she wanted me to say,
But I thought I'd state my name,
The way her jaw dropped as I spoke,
I'd finally had my say,

My heart was thumping out of my skin,
When she looked me in the eye,
I was determined not to say sorry,
Our friendship; has now died.

I now have found some new friends,
No more listening to her drone,
As I look across the playground,
She's standing on her own.

Hannah Whyburd (12)
Thurstable School

Love

My love is a fiery volcano
Ready to erupt and shock unknowing people;
It pounces like a cat to a mouse
And echoes through the minds of people nearby
Spreading and glowing, harming anything that gets in the way.
It isn't planned, it just happens.
My love is a fiery volcano: strong, tough, vicious.
It waits . . . waits until the time is right.
Then it explodes and bubbles slowly to houses and cities.
It hurts the small children tucked up in their cosy beds.
I cannot control it; it runs freely and uncontrollably,
Waving its sharp arms like a monkey in a zoo.
My love is a fiery volcano,
It must be caged and held back.
Because like the fiery volcano, it can do more than you know . . .

Bethany Dickinson (13)
Thurstable School

Permanent Tide

'Where are you going? What will you be?'
Unrelenting questions following me.
How should I know what the future holds
For a girl like me?
What to do and how to do it, they all know better than I
With my head in my hands
And a tear in my eye
All the pressure, the strain
No
Way
To
Release
It
Outside I smile, inside I am frowning
And I am not waving, my teacher
But drowning.

Suzanne Howes (15)
Thurstable School

Yellow Is

Yellow is a lily with lots of pollen.
Yellow is a Lamborghini sprayed yellow with stripes.
Yellow is a pencil case with a skull and crossbones.
Yellow is a post-it note with lots of stuff on it.
Yellow is a sun with a scorching temperature.
Yellow is a hot summer's day when it's boiling.
Yellow is a nice fluffy cushion.
Yellow is a mug with frogs on it.
Yellow is a jumbo jet with lightning bolts.
Yellow is a cat driving a car.
Yellow is a pencil, a yellow pencil.
Yellow is a sunflower with yellow petals.
Yellow is a poster with elephants on it.
Yellow is a lemon, a sour lemon.
Yellow is a bottle with fizzy water in it.
Yellow is lots of things.

David Owers (11)
Thurstable School

Silence

The wind blew silently,
Catching her hair,
Sighing. . . sitting . . thinking,
Does this always happen?
Why did she feel so lonely?
Watching her watch,
Tick from each minute,
She could hear the mournful cries,
She could see the black material,
And hear the vicar's cold, empty voice,
If only she hadn't had said, 'I hate you,'
If only it had been, 'I love you,'
A big reget,
But they're all gone now,
She was all alone,
Just like the beginning.

Jessica Vant (13)
Thurstable School

Family Always First

Always there, and always care,
Family always first.
Someone to love you, someone to help you,
Family always first.
Safe and sound I'm not alone,
I'm proud, happy to call this my home.
Easy to talk to, guaranteed to listen,
Family first, like stars they glisten.
Always understand, they proudly smile,
Watching me go that extra mile,
When I fall, you're always there,
You lend me a hand, I know you care.
Reassuring me, helping me out,
Never a moment, I have a doubt.
Life without them is not complete,
If they weren't around, my heart wouldn't beat.

Harriet Tsoi (13)
Thurstable School

My Sadness

My depression is a silent wave,
Constantly crashing into the golden sand,
Slowly picking away the fragments of towering cliffs and caves.
Washing away the memories that have been stored for years,
Washing away to the seabed where emotions and memories are left behind.

My misery is a serene meadow,
Gently swaying in the open breeze,
Growing with pain but elegance under the watery sky.
The bright fuscias and electric blues stick out among the plush grass.
The grass which sway us gently in the open breeze.

My sorrow is a cascading waterfall,
Trickling into a bottomless pit going nowhere.
Surrounded by flowers blossoming in the damp weather.
The constant flow of blue crystals pouring into an empty vase.
An empty vase that empty soon, to release a new emotion.

Ellen Blacow (13)
Thurstable School

Musical River . . .

My love is a musical river softly flowing.
It's sometimes quiet, it's sometimes loud.
Without a care in the world, it keeps flowing serenely, never stopping.
The water cascading down the hill
Singing its song,
Creating a melody of many notes,
Some high; yet some low.

Sometimes the river is crashing and rough,
Uncontrollable and unstoppable.
Yet sometimes it hardly flows at all.
The water soon starts gliding again,
Back to flow once more.

My river of love will always be there,
Never drying out,
It will keep singing its musical song.

Natasha Shade (13)
Thurstable School

Thank You!

Thank you for my hair,
Thank you for my nose,
Thanks for making me fair.

Thank you for my home,
Thanks for my best friend,
Thank you for my parents,
Although I drive them round the bend.

Thank you for my school,
Thank you for my food,
Not so many thanks for making me uncool.

I don't know who I'm thanking,
But I'll thank them anyway,
So I thank you for these things.
Thank you!

Thomas Bellotti (12)
Thurstable School

Bullying

Bullying is bad or is it good?
You know what the answer is
So do what you should.

Bullying is bad
Bullying is silly
So why do bullies bully?

Bullying is mean
Bullies can hurt
Bullies can be physical
And maybe more
Bullies can be mental
Bullies can be physical
Don't do anything
And you'll be just fine!

Molly Munson (11)
Thurstable School

Anti-Smoking

People seem to think it's great.
Even when they turn up late,
They think they're all too cool,
Acting big, bad and tall,
They want more and more,
Costing more and more.

Loitering around all over the place,
Chased all around, all over the place,
Police can't stop it,
Teachers can't stop it,
It's an epidemic, no one can stop it,
Spreading and spreading from kid to kid,
I won't back down
I'll stand my ground.

Sam Griffin (13)
Thurstable School

The Stars And The Sun

Yellow warm sun,
Like a golden bullet from a gun,
Goes across the sky,
Waiting to die.
The fireball coming to an end
Going round the bend,
Just to see its friend.

My shooting star,
As fast as a car.
Sparks fly off the side,
From the streets as it glides.
The star is bright,
As it speeds through the night
Coming back to tuck me in tight.

Jake Monk (11)
Thurstable School

What Bullying Can Do

She gets bullied every day,
Girl or boy, always the same.
Every day, every night always the same,
So she is smart, who cares?
Why does she have to feel the pain?

Now she is gone,
Left the school,
Why didn't she tell anyone?
What a fool.

So she was smart,
She was no bother.
She was not any of those words,
But a girl who's dead, buried in a coffin.

Lewis Johnson (12)
Thurstable School

Rabbit

Midnight,
And the rabbit is out enjoying his day
The nocturnal pest like a robber stealing cabbages in the night
But no one wakes and shoos him off
For his skill is to be silent.

Rabbit lives in a hole in the ground
Hidden within the hedge.
Within his hole is his home
Filled with things you and me own
Just in miniature.

Up comes the sun, rabbit's day has ended.
So he hops to his little bed to sleep till
Night comes again.

Jasmine Everett (11)
Thurstable School

Change

You can never change,
What's around you,
The sound, the theme,
The people who surround you.

Unlike me,
I can change my way,
As easy as it sounds,
It's harder than walking away.

My body shape shifts
The tingling sensation,
Awakens my day,
For my new life that lays
In front of me!

Cora Arrowsmith (13)
Thurstable School

My Box

(Inspired by 'Magic Box' by Kit Wright)

I will put in my box,
The daintiness of an autumn fairy as she dances flower to flower.
I will put in my box,
The crunch of an autumn leaf.
I will put in my box,
The tip of an icicle, as sharp as a pin.
I will put in my box,
My favourite scarf I was willing to put on my snowman
One late, frosty night.
I will put in my box,
The heat from the sun and the burn from the flame;
The dream I will fight to reach.

Kirby Taylor (11)
Thurstable School

The Beauty Of The Volcano

My love is for a fiery volcano, splattering lava in the air
Death to all it touches.
Life trembles in its power glaring at possible danger.
There is a certain beauty about the lava trickling between the crevasses,
Keeping in formation,
A satisfying hiss as it hits the water, causing it to turn to rock.
Images seem to stare back at you from the newly-formed stones.
The rocks fall to the ocean floor; fish explore the holes.
Coral forms around the soul of the rock.
Years pass; a diver swims near,.
Picks it up and leaves.
So now it is here, sitting on a mantelpiece
Staring into a strange new environment.

Shawn Cornish (13)
Thurstable School

Football

Kicking the ball as hard as I could,
Running as fast as my legs will carry me,
With the wind rushing through my hair,
Nothing can stop me except the goalie,
Looking in the direction I want to kick it,
I shoot,
As the goalie dives to try to stop it,
My hopes are held high,
It curls into the goal,
Straight into the back of the net,
I hear the roar of my team mates as they come running
Football is what I am,
What are you?

Matthew Khan (11)
Thurstable School

Black

Black is pure darkness with nothing in sight.
Black is emptiness with no feelings.
Black is the gloomy midnight sky,
Black is terrifying and makes people cry.
Black is a man with an empty heart.
He creeps up on you,
He hates you,
He is evil.
Black is space and gives you a fright.
Black is the evil inside of you.
Black is the sorrow that people show.
Black
Is nothing!

Maria-Ellen Carslake (11)
Thurstable School

Believe Me

Alone in my room, sat on my bed.
Her harsh words drumming inside my head:
'It's always you! Why do you lie?'
While *she* stands by the door, faking a cry.

Trust isn't an option, when my sister's around,
But her quiet, goody-two-shoes, in the wrong is never found.
Jumping to conclusion, no matter what's been done.
It's become her hobby, though for me it's never fun.

I'm just the puppet; while she writes the script.
There's a standing ovation, she wins over every critic.
Will you ever believe me? Can you hear my cries?
Take off the blindfold and open your eyes.

Hannah Kane (13)
Thurstable School

The Rain

The tears begin to fall, they come down, never-ending,
These are the cries of the sky, to the world the tears are descending.
The world seems to sparkle, but in a sad sort of way,
The world now looks different, so does each and every day.

The tears fall freely, they all land here and there,
On lips, on faces, on every strand of hair.
In puddles, on grass, on stones, in mud,
They land without a sound, no bang, or bash, or crash, or thud.

They sometimes cheer us up, or bring our mood right down,
They leave smiles on our faces, or sometimes make us frown.
I look up at the sky, my heart is filled with pain,
I hate the tears of the gods, which is commonly called the rain.

Katherine Read (13)
Thurstable School

Lucky

They've got it all,
All of the things I thought I wanted,
But I can't afford to fake anymore,
And I'll take all the things I've got for granted.

You think you are poor,
But you have got more than ever needed,
And you can't ignore, the things you have got,
Think of all those poor small kids that haven't.

Think what you've done,
Think of all the ways you spend your money,
And you can't afford to fake anymore,
Because you know that you are really lucky.

Bertie Rigby (12)
Thurstable School

The Big Mack

She's the girl with the most distinctive laugh
- That bellows down the corridor,
The one that always smiles at me,
Sometimes just because she knows I'm happy,
The one who cries when I cry,
Because she hates to see my pain.

She may be a weirdo,
Or even the loudest girl you know,
Perhaps even the funniest?
But to me,
She's more than any of that's,
Practically my sister - she's my best friend.

Kristie Smith (13)
Thurstable School

Bullying, What Is The Point Of It?

Bullying is a horrible thing,
Is it fun? Nobody knows.
Why do they do it? Nobody knows,
What sort of person makes a bully? Nobody knows.

Bullying is pointless, everybody knows.
It can be physical or verbal, everybody knows,
It can drive people mad, everybody knows.
It makes people angry, everybody knows.

Bullying is a horrible thing,
I'm scared and unhappy, nobody knows.
What will happen to me? Nobody knows.

Jamie Peachey (12)
Thurstable School

Colour Travels

I am a block of colour
A block of colour is me.
I can appear in your mind,
Because colour travels.
Brings emotions,
Flies like a parallel universe,
A phenomenon.
I am a block of colour
A block of colour is me,
I know your every will,
Because colour travels.

Thomas Crossley (11)
Thurstable School

I Loved That Balloon!

I loved that balloon, it was like no other,
And when it was with me, I would never suffer.
I loved that balloon, I would never let it go,
At one time I loved it so much,
I tied it to my toe.
I loved that balloon, I would never leave it behind,
Even when I lost it, it was never hard to find.
I loved that balloon it was my favourite balloon,
But one day I let it go and it drifted off to the moon.
I loved that balloon, I miss it so very much,
I can't believe I lost it, but I still love it very, very much!

Pele Heydon (13)
Thurstable School

My Amazing Mum

I love my mum so very much,
She's the warmth on my heart,
Whenever I see her she brightens up my day,
She always puts me first,
She never has time for herself,
Her love is greater than the flowers on a spring day,
And I'm proud to call her Mum,
She's very kind and loyal,
And very pretty too,
I love my mum and I would never change
A thing about her!

Michaela Richer (11)
Thurstable School

Midnight

In the darkness of midnight,
Bats coming out to bite
It looks like a white balloon,
The nice light comes from the moon.

A bat gliding in its flight,
It's flying like a kite,
With its yellow, bulging eyes,
Bats are creatures that lie.

In the trees it drinks cream tea,
It is silent like a bee.

Joshua French (11)
Thurstable School

Sometimes You See Him

Sometimes you see him sitting all by himself.
Sometimes you see him crying privately.
Sometimes you see him failing to fit in.
Sometimes you see him bunking off class.
Sometimes you see him being laughed at by us.
Sometimes you see him hiding where nobody knows.
This is what happened to him after being kicked out by us.
We don't realise he used to be one of us.
We haven't noticed this was all started by us.
We need to remember what we did.

Peter Greenwood (12)
Thurstable School

My Love Is . . .

My love is a glistening spring in the scorching desert
That burns faster than rubber on a racing car.

My love rolls by faster than lily clouds over serene, haunted mountainsides;
They echo every thought in mind.

My love is a rainbow, vibrant, luscious that lights up my life
Faster than the stars illuminate the darkness at night.

My love is an everlasting eternity, that is never going to end.
My love is my all; my all is my everything.

Emily Lane (13)
Thurstable School

My Love Is An Erupting Volcano

My love is an erupting volcano; all fiery and confused.
I feel like I cannot breathe, as the fire burns inside of me.
I keep on running, running away,
But I can't get far before it pulls me back in.

My love is like the red hot boulders tumbling down the mountainside,
As they reach the bottom they are free,
Free from the fire of the volcano.

Maddison Seaber (14)
Thurstable School

Teddy Bear

I love me teddy bear as he naps on me bed.
Cute little paws and a round little 'ead.
He gives me solace as bullets start to fly –
He gives me peace and a little place to cry.
As people sniff weed, I sniff 'is tummy.
Soft and plushy, smells like honey-
I drink juice while the thugs down rummy.
He is my mate and my best friend.
He is my shield as the world starts to end.

James Culley (13)
Thurstable School

I Don't Know Why

People think it's fine,
But they get addicted forever,
Some people say, 'Why?'
And some people say, 'Never.'

Some people can't resist,
They think they're big, bad and tall,
They begin to take more,
Right up to when they fall.

William Weller (13)
Thurstable School

The Old Willow Tree

The old willow tree is dark and misty,
Battered and bruised with curls and swirls.
The ancient roots all brown and twisty,
Just the sight could make a man hurt.

The old willow tree is at the bottom of the garden,
My grandma loves the old tree.
But she is so deaf all she says is 'Pardon?'
I look at the old willow tree as happy can be.

Charlie Hammond(13)
Thurstable School

Hallowe'en!

Hallowe'en is really scary
It's kind of weary too
Is there a vampire here or there?'
Argh!' look there's a bear!
What's happening?
Screaming and shouting 'Argh!'
Yet the best part is the
    Sweets!

Amy Georgina Lee Begg (11)
Thurstable School

The Wee Little Tree

The language in the day is different to it is at night,
The vision of the squirrel is different in light.
In the summer the heat keeps me warm,
My leaves are all in order and all in form.
In the winter my body is cold,
I lose all my leaves and now I become bald.
I stand here chilled and bored,
Night-night, I could snore!

Luke Gregory Towers (13)
Thurstable School

My Most Scariest Place

The sky is full of secrets, the sea full of fears,
Wherever you look or listen you'll be sure it will be near.
The ghosts that haunt the hallways, the birds that stare at me,
I'm sure I can hear footsteps, but nothing is what I see.
My heart is beating faster, the full moon in the sky,
As I wake up from my nightmare
I know my scare has passed me by.

Emma Dyer (12)
Thurstable School

Children In Need

You're paying some money to help others,
The people who can't have three meals a day,
The ones who live in a terrible place,
Unlike us, we live in a nice place,
We're so lucky we're not like them,
Give them some money so they can have a happy end.

You're paying some money to help others,
The people who can't have three meals a day,
They are the ones who live in a terrible place,
Unlike us, we are able to live with a smile on our faces.
We're so lucky we're not like them,
Give them some money so they can have a happy end.
Always be thoughtful and kind,
It doesn't matter where you are in the world,
Keep the less fortunate forever in your mind.

Luke James (11)
Thurstable School

Sometimes

Cats sometimes eat lemons in bed,
But don't let yourself be misled,
It's not what cats normally do,
Sometimes they visit the zoo,
And you can't help but feel a little in suspense,
Every time he jumps the garden fence.

Evangeline Perry (13)
Thurstable School

Squirrel

Feet worn to perfection,
Body slim,
Sharper than the breeze,
Tail bushier than the trees.

Stealth used to spy on passers-by and goers,
Speed taking skill to accelerate,
Leaps of faith, almost death defying,
Hidden,
Little,
Cuteness behind anger.

Oliver Mills (12)
Thurstable School

Bust-A-Rhyme - Essex

Young Writers Information

We hope you have enjoyed reading this book - and that you will continue to enjoy it in the coming years.

If you like reading and writing poetry drop us a line, or give us a call, and we'll send you a free information pack.

Alternatively if you would like to order further copies of this book or any of our other titles, then please give us a call or log onto our website at www.youngwriters.co.uk

Young Writers Information
Remus House
Coltsfoot Drive
Peterborough
PE2 9JX
(01733) 890066